JS
344
C5T7
1974

Toulmin
The city manager.

METROPOLITAN AMERICA

METROPOLITAN AMERICA

Advisory Editor
Richard C. Wade

Research Associate
Eugene P. Moehring

THE
CITY MANAGER
A NEW PROFESSION

HARRY AUBREY TOULMIN, Jr.

ARNO PRESS
A New York Times Company
New York / 1974

Reprint Edition 1974 by Arno Press Inc.

Copyright © 1915 by D. Appleton and Company
Reprinted by permission of Hawthorn Books, Inc.

Reprinted from a copy in the
Newark Public Library

METROPOLITAN AMERICA
ISBN for complete set: 0-405-05380-0
See last pages of this volume for titles.

Manufactured in the United States of America

Library of Congress Cataloging in Publication Data

Toulmin, Harry Aubrey, 1890-
    The city manager.

    (Metropolitan America)
    Reprint of the ed. published by D. Appleton, New York, in series: National Municipal League series.
    Bibliography: p.
    1. Municipal government by city manager--Vocational guidance. I. Title. II. Series. III. Series: National Municipal League monograph series.
JS344.C5T7 1974   352'.0084'023   73-11936
ISBN 0-405-05428-9

THE CITY MANAGER

The
National Municipal League Series
EDITED BY
CL'NTON ROGERS WOODRUFF
Secretary of the National Municipal League

City Government by Commission
Edited by CLINTON ROGERS WOODRUFF

The Regulation of Municipal Utilities
Edited by CLYDE LYNDON KING

The Initiative, Referendum and Recall
Edited by WILLIAM BENNETT MUNRO

The Social Center
By EDWARD J. WARD

Woman's Work in Municipalities
by MARRY RITTER BEARD

Lower Living Costs in Cities
By CLYDE LYNDON KING

The City Manager
By HARRY AUBREY TOULMIN, JR.

Satellite Cities
By GRAHAM R. TAYLOR

City Planning
Edited by JOHN NOLEN

D. APPLETON AND COMPANY
Publishers   New York

NATIONAL MUNICIPAL LEAGUE SERIES

THE
CITY MANAGER
A NEW PROFESSION

BY

HARRY AUBREY TOULMIN, Jr.
J.D., F.S.S.
Author of "Social Historians"

NEW YORK AND LONDON
D. APPLETON AND COMPANY
1916

COPYRIGHT, 1915, BY
D. APPLETON AND COMPANY

PRINTED IN THE UNITED STATES OF AMERICA

To
HON. JAMES M. COX
Conspicuous Leader
in
Constructive Citizenship
This Narrative of
Progress
is
Dedicated

INTRODUCTION

The city manager, or as some who prefer to suggest the continuity of the development in the title call it, the commission-manager form of government, has achieved a wide reputation in a very short time. To some this seems surprising, but the reasons are obvious to those who have followed closely the development of municipal charter reform: It represents the product of many years of thoughtful consideration of the whole subject and of the increased appreciation of the dignity and power of the worth of city government and the need for experts in administering it. A generation ago the people were indifferent to the importance of municipal government. They have gradually but none the less surely been awakened from their lethargy and are beginning to appreciate that city government is one of the great factors in human life and bids fair to become even a greater factor during coming generations. With the dawning appreciation of the importance of municipal government came an appreciation of the fact that our municipal machinery was hopelessly involved and complicated and inadequate.

Then began the movement for new charters, which has run a varied course, but has really had a very definite single purpose, namely, that of simplification, and through the elimination of unnecessary machinery and the unification of power and responsibility in the hands of a single board of conspicuous men who were responsive as well as responsible to the electorate. The part which the movement for commission government has followed in this movement is familiar to the members of the National Municipal League and to the readers of its Proceedings, the *National Municipal Review* and of the National Municipal League Series.

This form of government, introduced in the storm-stricken city of Galveston, on the Gulf of Mexico, was designed to prepare the American municipal mind for the next important step, namely, that of concentrating the administration of the city in the hands of a qualified expert in municipal government. Coincident with the commission government movement was the awakening of public interest in municipal affairs and the movement to prepare the American municipal citizen to demand that municipal offices should be taken out of politics and be open to those who were willing to devote their lives to municipal service and who had demonstrated their fitness so to do.

INTRODUCTION

Mr. Toulmin's volume on the city manager adequately sets forth the details of the city manager form of government as it exists in a score of our cities and how it is actually working out in these communities. As a citizen of Dayton, as an interested citizen as well as a student, he has had ample opportunity to study at first hand the city manager form of government, and he has availed himself of the opportunity. Moreover, he had had the advantage of consultation and close contact with those who were making the experiment. The results of his study, experience and observation are embodied in this volume, which we believe will form not only an important addition to the National Municipal League Series, but aid in the development of sound public opinion upon this very important question.

CLINTON ROGERS WOODRUFF.

CONTENTS

CHAPTER		PAGE
I.	FOREWORD	1
II.	THE OLD ORDER	6
III.	PRELIMINARY PLANS	16
IV.	THE POWER OF THE ELECTORATE	36
V.	THE NEW COMMISSION	51
VI.	THE CITY MANAGER	73
VII.	THE DEPARTMENTS	98
VIII.	FINANCE MEASURES	123
IX.	EDUCATION OF OFFICIALS	146
X.	ATTITUDE OF LABOR AND SOCIALISM TOWARD THE CITY MANAGER PLAN	155
XI.	CITY MANAGER STATUTES	170
XII.	RESULTS	194
XIII.	VARIOUS POINTS OF VIEW	223
XIV.	ADVANTAGES AND DISADVANTAGES	255
APPENDIX A.	CITY GOVERNMENT BY COMMISSION; A REPORT OF THE NATIONAL MUNICIPAL LEAGUE	268
APPENDIX B.	CITIES UNDER THE CITY MANAGER PLAN, JUNE 1, 1914	281
APPENDIX C.	SOME ACID TESTS OF CITY MANAGER GOVERNMENT FROM THE FIRST NINETY DAYS OF OPERATION	282
APPENDIX D.	PLEDGE CARD AND PRECINCT CARD	287
APPENDIX E.	BIBLIOGRAPHY	289
INDEX		299

LIST OF DIAGRAMS

	PAGE
Staunton, Va., Controlled Executive Plan	20
Lockport, New York, Proposal	22
Old Plan in Dayton	58
City Manager Plan, Dayton, Ohio	75
Hickory, N. C., City Manager Plan	88
Springfield, Ohio, City Manager Plan	113

THE CITY MANAGER

CHAPTER I

FOREWORD

Now this is nothing short of a new social age, a new era of human relationships, a new stage setting for the drama of life. WOODROW WILSON

City government is experiencing a civic revolution. We have run suddenly upon a novel age where well-tried formulas are nil, where old landmarks are transformed into strange beacon lights, and the new anchorage we all seem to be seeking is yet afar off. Revolution in municipal government is but one of our ventures into the virgin land of untried things. The seeking of the truer and the cleaner and the finer, of the less wasteful and of the more efficient, is the advertisement of our national restlessness. The failure of the old has stung our pride into a pilgrimage to find something newer, nobler, more satisfying than that which the old government could give with its incompetence, its sloth, its extravagance. This discussion has as its sole excuse the object of presenting a part of the progress of our recent political life.

A word then as to the point of view.

It is trite, perhaps, to say that this is the age of specialists and professional men. Nevertheless, what is here written is an exposition of that truism. It is profoundly believed that a vast part of a city's business must be run by a man experienced in municipal administration. This is not so much the dream of the visionary as it is the persuasion of practical minds facing the glaring facts of civic failures. While cities do not go into the hands of a receiver as easily as do corporations and individuals, yet the same bankrupt condition often exists without that salutary relief. Professional administrators are proposed as the remedy and the preventive. What is here written is expository of the professional idea in municipal life, its method and advantage and the opportunities open to its practice.

The church, law, medicine, and other professions may boast of professional emoluments and rewards. This newcomer in the ranks equals any one of the distinguished predecessors in its offer of startling opportunities for genuine constructive service by its personnel, for the achievement of personal repute, and for accomplishment by them of finer things.

FOREWORD

We are about to learn a new meaning of the dignity of public service and acquire a new conception of civic ethics. To this end we will direct ourselves.

All goodness in government is achieved by evolution, not simply by invention. The original systems of municipal government will often be referred to herein as the "old order"; the city manager plan with all its attendant progressive features and ideals will be referred to as the "new order." Between the two is no hard and fixed boundary upon which to lay your finger and say it is there, and to the one side is one thing, and to the other is another. Those things produced by evolution inevitably have shadowed beginnings and endings.

So it is in municipal government. The old order was first a rule with the usual mayor and council, often composed of two branches. Then Galveston popularized the commission government with no mayor. In a little more than a decade we saw many pleasing modifications of this plan; the process was slow, but the leaven was at work in the loaf. Thus matters had evolved in the old order up to nineteen hundred and eleven.

From this genesis the new order sprang. The city manager plan is a part of this more modern trend of thought. Many earnest thinkers are persuaded that it is a step further forward toward the realization of true civic greatness. While time alone can adequately answer this question, in the meanwhile, to understand the import of it and the deep significance it bears upon the life of modern municipalities, it is not out of place to give the plan the careful thought resultant from the mature deliberation which it deserves. Throughout what is said hereafter it will be understood that when no reference is made to a particular charter, when a provision of some charter is being discussed, it is assumed by the writer that it is a part of the instrument under which Dayton (Ohio) is governed. This is done for the reason that the most unique instrument dealing with the city manager is the charter of Dayton, and the discussion of the city manager plan logically hinges about the advanced position this charter assumes.

One word as to the history of this movement. It has been a matter of comment quite frequently that Europe had the essence of the plan already in effective operation. This is neither literally nor substantially true. The idea abroad was only partially formulated before it was fully developed in this country, and, in fact, still remains but partially formulated there. All credit for so radical an achievement belongs to the American people who actually created it. A full analysis and discussion of these so-called progenitors are set forth at length in the later part of this sketch.

A final word in passing. So far as this exposition of the city manager plan of city government creates an interest in it and clarifies the discussion of it in the minds of the people who vote upon the plan, who rule by and under the provisions embodied in a city manager charter, who will be officials charged with its execution and success, so far will this narrative justify its existence. Usefulness will be the test of its worth.

CHAPTER II

THE OLD ORDER

The basis of our political systems is the right of the people to make and to alter their constitutions of government.   GEORGE WASHINGTON

The Indictment.—We want a change. American city government has had a multitude of grievous charges laid at its door. Numbers of these accusations were unjust, but far too many counts of the indictment have been sustained. Instituted to serve the citizen, too often has the city organization been the harbinger of those who robbed the people by their corruption and inefficiency. These are stinging charges to substantiate against our institutions of administration, but even the most callow enthusiast must admit the fallacies in our systems of municipal management. Such is the situation. We must face it and conquer it and alleviate it. Here, then, follows a relation of the most advanced remedy for these evils in the shape of the city manager plan. It is not a panacea for all ills, nor the sovereign solvent of every difficulty in city affairs, but it has at least to recommend it the sincere labor of able men who framed the charters and the indorsement of practical administrators.

Amateurs v. Professionals.—Undoubtedly true, as it is, that the old commission form of municipal government, originating in Galveston, has enacted many signally excellent measures, yet it has not proven the "cure-all" its advocates expected. Under this new régime, in so many cases, the old style of office-holder has wormed his way back into positions of power. The new duties and new responsibilities and enthusiasms of the hour, arising in the change from the mayor and council plan to the stock commission government, have done much to regenerate the job of public city office. The original commission plan has much to recommend it, but it is found to be not the ultimate nor next to the ultimate phase of municipal administration. The vital error still remains in the commission form of city government—that amateurs are called upon to execute what only the professionally experienced are competent to perform.

The Solution.—How are we to secure the benefit of such experience? The answer to this is contained in those advanced instruments of government, the city charters embodying the city manager plans. Many cities are considering following those conspicuous examples of leadership exhibited by cities adopting the *city* manager idea. To those cities contemplating a change, then, and to all those citizens interested in the live issues in modern municipalities, what follows will be of keenest interest. It relates a chapter in civic progress.

The Rise of the New City.—Twice, out of an appalling catastrophe, came new cities: first, Galveston, then Dayton. Efforts had already been made in the latter city, looking to a change of government prior to that fateful flood morning in March, 1913. In the gray hours of earliest dawn, under the soaking valley mists, a mud-laden sea, seven inches deep over four hundred square miles of watershed, poured down the Miami Valley, rose above the crumbling levies around the city, and lifted its foaming front step by step into the heart of the helpless town—with dawn came terror, with daylight destruction, with midnight the highwater-mark of pitiless devastation.

The city of Dayton stood neck deep in the icy current. Snow and sleet and rain soaked what would have remained dry above the sea; no light, no food, no dry land—and assets by the millions hourly following each other into nothingness. Then dawn broke again; now there was no law, no government, no supreme power except the courage of the citizens. The disease of destruction broke out in fire, and what the flood refused to take was sacrificed in flame, rising in smoke to the steaming heavens. This was picturesque and dramatic and inhuman. But the terrible toll was only beginning to be taken.

Then the aftermath. The old government was suspended. Military rule guided by a commission of citizens took its place: like Galveston, a group of able men brought the chaos in Dayton into precisive order. Out of the old was born the new. Traditions, old ideals, habits, venerable customs foregathered with their fathers, for a new lesson in the meaning of efficiency of government and concentrated power and organization had been taught. It was the vision of genuine civic greatness. The new government now is a step toward the realization of that constructive purpose.

The Turning Point.—This catastrophe was the second milestone in the evolution of city government. Curiously, disasters have been the landmarks of municipal progress. The efficiency of the Citizens' Relief Committee, acting as a commission, gave the people of Dayton confidence in a newer form of government.

Dayton wanted efficiency, and knowledge of herself was the first step to secure it. Exact, scientific, painstaking knowledge must be the working basis of all genuine constructive social service. And this type of information we must take to be the price of all good government; it demands laborious genius, eager to take infinite pains, to learn the truth about a city so that a fitting remedy can be applied.

That was the genus of the genius which Dayton had. She took stock of herself and found that the old city government had three disastrous faults. First, its financial system was entirely antiquated. There was no set procedure for the formulation of a scientific budget; there was no accurate system of cost, or operating records; there was no up-to-date accounting system. A haphazard spirit of ignorant inefficiency dominated the whole civic organization. Second, there was no genuine merit system whereby the personnel could be selected upon a basis of fairness and equality. Third, the Department of Health was in a pitifully inefficient state, through no fault of the managing officers, but by reason of the fact that the whole organization of the department and the method of managing it were completely out of accord with the spirit and object of a bureau of health. The departments of Fire and Police were suffering from a similar disorganization.

Government by Deficit.—By this phrase the Dayton Bureau of Research cleverly dubbed the old government. It was a government by deficit, a government with no check on expenditure by any department, with little forethought in regard to that embarrassing future question as to where the money was to come from.

The Shame of a City.—In six years the total deficit amounted to $360,000, or an average of $60,000 a year; in 1912 alone the council made the barefaced appropriation of $1,051,300 upon an acknowledged income of the city of $943,000, or an excess over income of $108,300. The debt of Dayton increased from $26.37 per capita in 1903 to $46.13 per capita in 1913; an increase of 76 per cent. in ten years. The annual tax income of the city in 1913 was $984,321.00, yet $452,378.00 was spent in the liquidation of maturing bonds and interest—47 per cent. of the total income was thus disbursed to carry the indebtedness incurred during the past by mismanagement and other causes.

The city was kept going by issuing bonds. The real remedy should have been to eliminate the expense and extravagance which produced the deficit; yet that was not the worst of it. These bonds were issued for expenditures which represented current expenses, not permanent improvements. To issue bonds for a permanent improvement of substantial life and some durability, with a provision for a sinking fund which should equal the amount of interest and principal upon maturity of bonds, would be sound finance. To issue bonds for current expenses or matters of very short life, long since passed out of existence when the bonds mature, is nothing less than financial suicide. Dayton, like many another city, has been doing that very thing.

Apropos of this, the Research Bureau published during the campaign for the new charter, a series of startling tables and graphic charts. They were vigorous arguments for a civic revolution. Here is one of them on the subject of issuing bonds:

Amount Still Outstanding	Purpose	Year of Issue	Year of Last Payment	Estimated Life of Improvement
$108,000	Unpaid bills and payrolls	1909	1924	None
25,000	Street lighting	1911	1940	None
30,000	Street lighting	1911	1925	None
50,000	Street repairs	1911	1935	5 years
13,000	Street repairs	1905	1925	5 years
100,000	Paving	1894	1916	10–15 years
175,000	Paving	1893	1919	10–15 years
15,000	Cleaning sewers	1908	1926	None
25,000	Reissue street paving (should have been paid at maturity, 1911)	1894	1927	10–15 years

This table speaks for itself.

In the face of these pregnant facts, the outgoing

council in 1913 voted a general increase of salary for between ninety and one hundred officials and employees, aggregating $27,990 additional per year for the long-suffering taxpayers to provide for. These increases were not to compensate unusual merit or increased efficiency or additional labor. It was a part of a policy to relegate economy to the forgotten arts.

The population of Dayton between 1903 and 1913 increased 35,000. The debt increased during that period of a decade $757,800.

The usual difficulties with the old form of government had practically bankrupted the city of Dayton in contrast to the personal prosperity of its citizens. On December 24, 1912, there was $900,000 of municipal money in bank, bearing 3 per cent. interest; nevertheless on that day, private citizens paid the firemen and policemen of a force much reduced in numbers. An unwieldy charter and a long period of consequent inefficiency presented a city bankrupt with exactly $911,712.42 of unreachable funds.

The Question.—So, after all, the problem presented to Dayton was a business problem. Cities are vast businesses, and all face what Dayton faced. Put the question confronting the citizens in a business way. Suppose one of those persuasive gentlemen (who sell industrial stock) were to try to sell you shares in a corporation with an annual payroll of nearly a half-million, plus a bonded debt which demanded nearly a half-million more yearly to meet the interest on it and to retire it, making a rough million a year in disbursements; and suppose further that the president could practically negative all the acts of the directors and the directors could and did vote money for corporate uses without regard to income, and that supplies were bought as anybody pleased, and that stockholders were practically unable to inspect the books, or if they could, the books were unintelligible to all but expert accountants. Further than this, take into consideration that this public corporation had a yearly deficit of nearly 10 per cent. of its disbursements, and a total debt of *nearly seven millions.* Then, realizing all this, would you invest your capital, your energy, your family's happiness and even safety in such a wildcat venture of commercial insecurity?

You would not! Yet that was how the public corporation of Dayton stood. No more shame to Dayton than to a dozen lesser and greater cities, but more credit to her now for her courageous remedy of the matter.

City Manager Waite was quoted as saying, upon a thorough examination of the city situation, "What

Dayton needs is a receiver instead of a manager."

But what Dayton got was a manager. This was his problem—the regeneration of a municipal business; and what is said hereafter is an exposition of the means of his accomplishing it.

CHAPTER III

PRELIMINARY PLANS

The conduct of a people under given circumstances must always be powerfully affected by the view which it takes of its mission and destiny.

JAMES BASSET MOORE

FIRST AMERICAN MANAGER PLANS

STAUNTON PLAN.—January 13, 1908, saw the passage of a measure, by a city council in a little Virginia city, of profound import to American municipal life. The town of Staunton desired commission government and inspired by the radical advantages Galveston and other cities had achieved, it was eager to adopt a similar program.

A barrier stood in the way. The state constitution contained the mandatory provision that all cities of the first class must have a mayor and council. This was a blank legal wall to overcome, for in Staunton there lived over 12,000 people. It was therefore indisputably a city of the first class. But some genius discovered that the power to appoint new officers by the council was particularly set forth in Section 1038 of the Virginia Code. Depending on this vantage point, an ordinance was passed, providing for a general manager, equipped with power to take entire charge and control of all the executive work of the city in its various departments, and entire charge and control of the heads of departments and employees of the city. The general manager under that plan assumed all executive duties, except those reserved to the finance, ordinance, school and auditing committees. It will thus be seen that finance, education, and legislation were properly withheld from his control, the latter power obviously out of his sphere and the former power retained wisely in order to constitute a check upon his actions.

This new executive was appointed by council for a definite term of one year at a salary of $2,000 (now $2,500). The new manager was financial adviser of the council, a court to hear complaints of citizens, and supervisor of the superintendents of highways, parks, lights, water, and corrections. He was made the purchasing agent, eliminating the heterogeneous, ill-advised and wasteful miscellaneous buying by each petty department and substituting a business-like standardized policy of wholesale, low-price purchasing. The manager in this form is more nearly a "controlled executive" than in the later city manager plans; in Staunton expenditures of $100 or over must be approved by council and then audited by the council's auditing committee before the fund is expended; the manager has no power to contract loans, or fix tax rates, or formulate policies, or supervise the police and fire departments, for they are under the control of the mayor, although he purchases for these latter departments. The books of the city are not only open to the public for inspection at will, but are so kept that the financial condition of the city can be ascertained daily.

As Hon. John Crosby, President of the Common Council in Staunton, says: "Neither the people nor the council have surrendered any of their sovereign rights; they have simply created an office known as that of a general manager, a paid employee, who devotes his whole time and attention to the business of the city and who is responsible to the council and the people, instead of intrusting the affairs of the city to the committees of the council." This is an adroit way of stating the new doctrine of civic power. He says further: "For each councilman thinks that the other members of the committee have more time than he has for looking after the business of the city, and each committeeman is of the same opinion—always willing to let the other fellow do it. As a result, that which is everyone's business is no one's business, and the poor old city gets along the best she can to the detriment of the taxpayer in particular and the people in general." This epitome of the old spirit of our public officers is well and pointedly put. And this is a plan whose innovation did not cause an increase in bonded debt nor a rise in the tax rate, although during the very period of its introduction the productive saloon license, amounting to $12,500, was taken from the city's income, and several disasters of several times that amount caused a heavy drain on the city's finances.

The city manager idea has been a distinct improvement and success in Staunton. True as it was that the city manager plan was yet to be developed in its entirety, nevertheless Staunton had the basic idea and pioneered the innovation despite risk and ridicule. To Staunton then goes the laurels for the first practical application of a business manager scheme to civic affairs.

LOCKPORT PROPOSAL.—A bill was introduced into the New York Legislature in 1911 setting forth what was known as the "Lockport Plan." The idea was that by means of a general enabling act, which could be applied to any third-class city through local action, a particular form of charter could be adopted

STAUNTON, VA., CONTROLLED EXECUTIVE PLAN

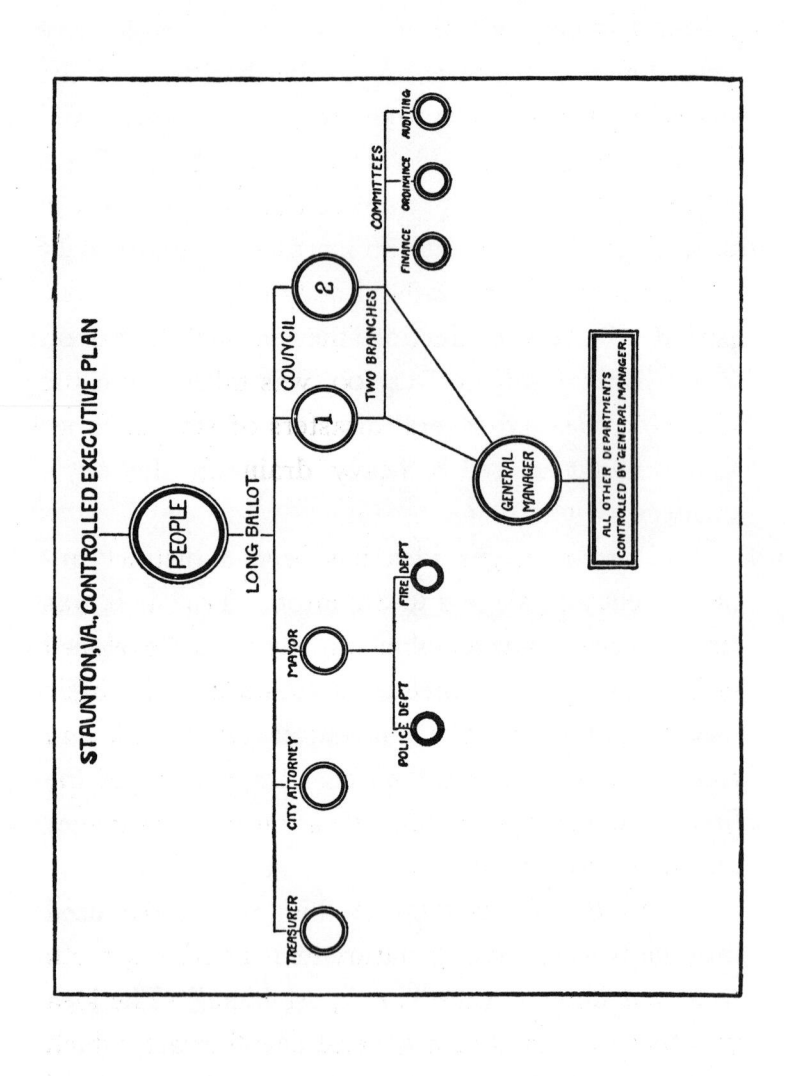

which would allow the city to appoint a chief executive who would manage the public corporation as the general manager of a private corporation would do. This plan had for its basic idea the conferring of the fundamental powers of initiative and referendum and recall upon the people. Through the agency of a short ballot a council of four members and a presiding officer termed a mayor would be elected. There would be a board of education elected. The council would appoint a city manager who, in turn, would have all power of appointment and removal of officers not specifically provided for in the proposed charter.

This city council was to have a limited amount of control over the administrative department in this wise: First, it could issue general and special orders, by resolution, to the city manager to give him authority to carry out the powers and duties conferred upon him; second, it was to require the city manager to file with it a complete report of the condition of the departments once a year and miscellaneous separate reports of a special nature at any intervening time; third, the city council was furthermore to constitute a board of estimate and apportionment in those cases where such board was provided for; fourth, the city council could also provide a board of audit, independent

LOCKPORT, NEW YORK, PROPOSAL

PEOPLE
INITIATIVE REFERENDUM RECALL PROTEST
SHORT BALLOT
COUNCIL
MAYOR
BOARD OF EDUCATION
BOARD OF AUDIT
CITY MANAGER

MANAGER APPOINTS AND REMOVES ALL OFFICERS NOT SPECIFICALLY PROVIDED FOR.

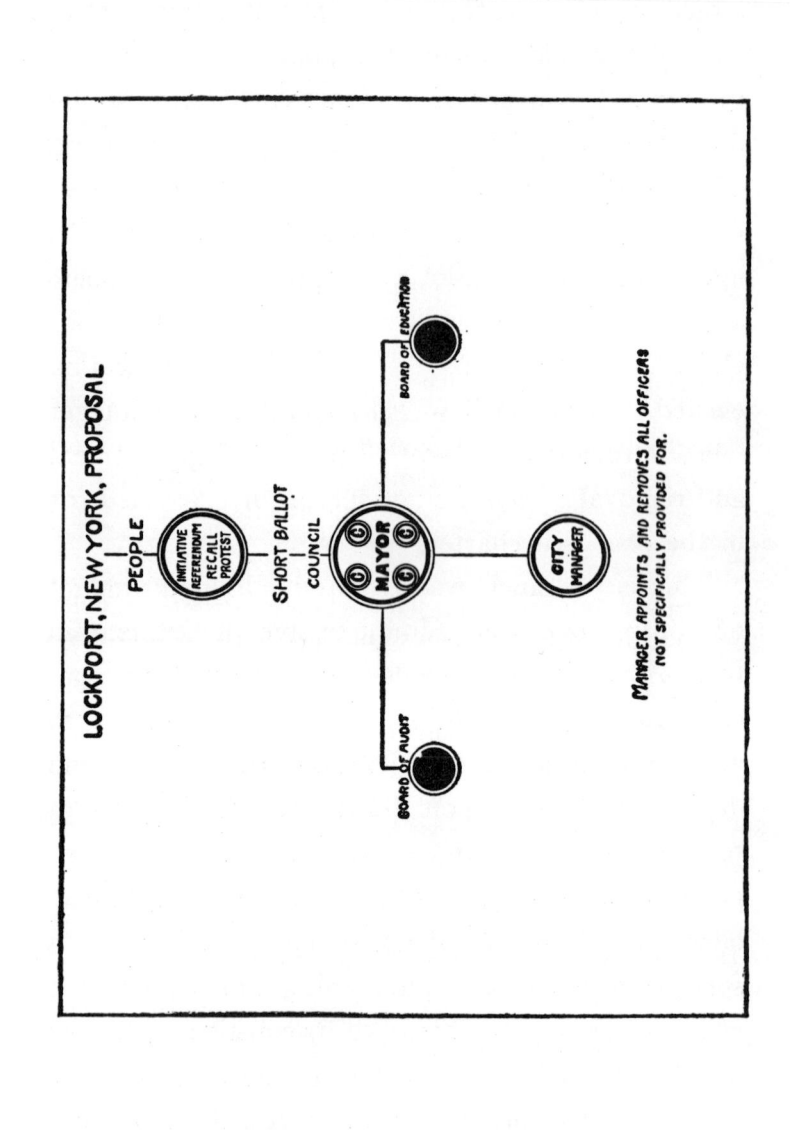

of the city manager, which was to have ready access to the vouchers and records of the administrative departments, with the exception of the claims arising from personal injury to property as these were to be passed upon by the city council itself; fifth, the city council was to have the power to validate whatever lawful acts were performed by the administrative officer of the city when he acted without any previous authority; sixth, in cities where highway districts were independent, the city council members were to be *ex officio* commissioners of highways.

The city manager under this proposal would have peculiar powers. He would be administrative head of the government. His tenure of office was to be at the pleasure of the city council. He was to exercise the general powers of executing laws and ordinances promulgated by the city council. He was to do whatever was conferred upon mayors of cities. He was to make proper recommendations and reports, and advise as to finances and other material matters relative to the city's welfare. He was to appoint all the officers whose selection was not provided for in some other fashion. He was to designate officers to perform certain duties which the council had ordered performed, and to give written notice to heads of the departments to transact business suggested by the council. He was to sign documents as the public agent of the city and have access to all the books and vouchers of the city; he was to have power to conduct whatever examination of officials or conditions which might be necessary for a thorough knowledge of the public business which it was vital for him to have.

This was, therefore, the first complete city manager plan proposed.

The European Method of Municipal Government

FOREIGN IDEAS.—Europe is credited with a large share of the honor in originating novel forms of city government. The Continent has been awarded the distinction of the creation of the essentials of the city manager plan of municipal rule, but it has been given too large a meed of praise in view of the actual facts of the case. The renown for the real development and the genuine creation of this most novel of municipal governments should be awarded to the genius of the American people.

GERMAN CITY GOVERNMENT.—The government of Prussian cities is often cited as the leading example of the application of the idea of a city manager to municipal affairs. In a measure this is true. There does exist in German cities a profession of expert administrators, who as members of the Magistrat or as Bürgermeisters have formed a large class of municipal officials. Nor must the members of the various councils be neglected in the enumeration of those who take part in the administration of German city governments.

A brief survey of the Prussian Municipal Government will be of value in understanding the exact status of the expert administrator abroad. The chiefest executive power is exercised by a body of men called a Magistrat. The Magistrat is an administrative council, composed of a number of administrators, one or two of whom are entitled Bürgermeisters.

Bürgermeister.—This official is the chief administrative officer and presiding figure at the meeting of the Magistrat; but he is distinctly the colleague of the fellow-members of the Magistrat and not their superior officer. While he may be the chief magistrate of the city and the ceremonial head of the local government, he is not the all-powerful executive whom no one can gainsay. There is no power of veto in him. He is selected by the city council from a number of candidates without regard to his place of residence, but solely with an eye to his past record for achieving results in the administration of city affairs. He must be preëminently a clear-headed, vigorous executive with capacity and talent for municipal work and equipped with a generous technical training. His is a profession in which advancement is based upon the achievement of actual results, so that he may expect to rise from smaller to larger cities according as he demonstrates his ability to successfully discharge the duties imposed upon him. It is a life work with him and the smallness of salary is in a large measure compensated for by the honor and social prestige and permanence of office as well as the generous pension which will be his upon the discharge of his duties for a greater or less period of time. He is, as Professor Munro aptly states him to be, "an expert, a professional administrator, who looks upon his office as a career, who seeks the post on his public record, and who expects promotion upon this alone."

Term of Office: Salary.—His term of office is usually twelve years. In cities the size of Leipsic and Dresden he may be appointed for life. If he serves his first twelve years, a second term of similar length is very sure to follow; and upon the completion of the service of twelve years his pension will be half-pay, and if he discharges his duties for twenty-four years, his pension will be nearly full pay. His salary is not one which is of any material size, as we are proposing to pay our city managers or even have paid our mayors. In Germany, the Bürgermeister enjoys a great security of office; in America, the city manager occupies a very precarious position subject as he is to the quondam whim of the electorate exercising their powers of recall as they please. Many times there is a considerable advantage to the Bürgermeister by virtue of the fact that he is allowed an official residence. His expenses are few to keep up his position for he is not compelled to spend a large amount in humoring his political followers and in assisting constituents and in financing campaigns and indulging in public projects, such as charities which customarily form a great drain upon the resources of American officials.

Powers and Duties.—As to his function in government, the Bürgermeister is primarily the presiding officer at all meetings of the Magistrat. He carries into effect the directions of that body and is the executive agent who makes effective the orders of the administrators. He supervises all the actual detail work of the numerous municipal officers, yet he makes no appointments of any importance. His is the duty to divide among the proper joint commissions the "various departments of civic administration" and his is the problem to select the personnel of these commissions from the citizen deputies, the council and the Magistrat. He has the additional authority to inspect the various municipal departments, and where the police administration is not vested wholly in the State, he has some control over that. It is to be understood, however, that the detail work of police administration is always vested in a police commissioner whenever the control of that force is wholly civic in character.

Character of Magistrat.—The Magistrat is composed of a number of able men who are experts in municipal administration. Some of the members are paid and some unpaid. In size it may be a board of considerable magnitude, running in number as high as thirty-four in the larger cities. The members are selected by the city council for a period of twelve years, usually, but in some cases even for life. This provision applies to paid members only as the unpaid members are elected for one-half of the twelve-year term.

Departments.—These paid Magistrats are expert administrators to each of whom is assigned a particular department of the city's affairs. The department may be that of education, of law, of public work, of hospital service, or of finance. The division into departments is very nearly akin to what we have in America. To become a departmental head it is necessary to have a particular training, often highly technical in character, and have an adequate experience to discharge the functions of that division of government to which the particular official is assigned. There is seldom seen, therefore, the anomalous condition of American city management where a man, fitted by training and technical knowledge for the administration of one department of government, inexperienced in any other, is put in control of a division totally alien to his talents. In Prussia, the selection of an official is based upon the same method that we use in the selection of a business manager or a purchasing agent for a large private corporation.

Powers of Magistrat.—The unpaid members of the Magistrat are chosen because of their general administrative ability. They must be residents of the city, but beyond that there is no requirement as to their qualifications save that general one. Professor Munro has performed a most illuminating service in his late book on "The Government of European Cities" in the classification of the powers of the Magistrat, briefly as follows:

The Magistrat must execute the national laws. Upon it devolves the duties of preparing business for the council and the execution of their joint measures. Supervision of municipal activities rests upon the Magistrat. The members of the board must completely administer all matters of revenue, both income and outgo. This body is charged with the care of all property which the city owns. They appoint all the paid officers of the city and this is a very important power for only the material officers are paid officers; they also have the power of removal and determine the salaries of the officials. They are guardians and caretakers of all public documents, as well as private documents. They are the official representatives of the city. They apportion the work among the authorities and officials who do the actual detail work of the city.

Council.—The third material division in German city government is the council. It is a slow-moving deliberative body, usually about three times as large as the Magistrat and composed of a large number of influential and powerful men whose wisdom is employed to formulate policies for the welfare of the city, and who serve as a check upon the actual performances of the Magistrat over whom they have appointive power. Its dual functions are as advisory board to the Magistrat and as a legislative body, passing upon the proposals of the administrative department. The budget is the crucial proposal every year and that is the one about which the chief interest centers. The council's domain of power is even extended to the initiation of measures; nevertheless, this is usually performed by the Magistrat. The meetings of this legislative body are very formal and very tedious, but, in spite of the amount of red tape which seems to burden its actions, it is a useful and serviceable organ of government. Indeed, it is doubtless an institution of great value in German city life; yet, like many other foreign ideas when transplanted to our soil, it would probably prove wholly unsuited to us and disastrous in consequence.

HISTORY REPEATS ITSELF.—The ills of the modern American city are but the repetition of the pitiful condition of English cities in the eighteenth century when the Royal Commission of 1833 was first empowered to investigate the affairs of the boroughs. That Commission found a startling state of affairs. Yet the conditions then were scarcely worse in an administrative way than our own affairs in many American cities of the present, and the conditions existed then with far better excuse than we can present now in more modern times.

The English town clerk has been said to be the progenitor of the city manager. This is an erroneous assumption. The only way in which the English town clerk or any of the English officials in municipal government have any similarity or relation to the present modern form of municipal American government lies in the fact that the English officer is usually a highly trained individual, commonly a professional man, who regards his position with the city as a part in a profession. It is so much of a profession that young men are "articled" to town clerks, then go out themselves to serve as town clerks in small cities, and gradually rise to higher positions in larger cities as their abilities may justify.

The town clerk is the chief legal officer of the municipality. He is in large measure an executive officer of professional character, an adviser to the council and a representative of the municipality in many city affairs involving technical legal problems. So far as his duties extend, he is, therefore, a professional administrator and in that regard is a counterpart of the city manager. But he does not have entire control of the city, and entire responsibility for all departments with power of appointment and power of removal. He only exercises jurisdiction over a particular section of municipal government, there being a number of other officials, all of whom must coact with him and each of whom has his share in contributing toward the final result of efficiency or inefficiency, as the case may be.

The council in English cities is a very important

and influential body whose actions and opinions are entitled to the greatest consideration and weight. Its say is paramount. Its members may disregard the advice of the technical heads of various departments who work under them and their committees; this is unusual, but it may be done and illustrates the entire freedom with which they exert their powers.

In this slight regard, therefore, it will be seen that the English city has only the germ of the idea which is embodied in the modern American city government. It has the idea of a well-trained technical man, who, by profession, is a municipal expert and administrator, devoting his life to it as professional work and expecting to remain in it for its corresponding rewards of honor and recompense.

The salaries of the town clerks are not always very large, but the various side emoluments of the office are such that they attract to the position men of unusual worth and very high qualifications. There are the identical inducements which attract to German municipal life the finest of the technical administrators in the Empire. The position is made attractive not only for its salary, but for its honor and reputation and the power and respect accorded it. These will have to become material elements in the success of the American plan. High qualities in the administrator and unusual services cannot be secured by exorbitant salaries only; but much must be done and much must be secured by instilling into the atmosphere of the place a certain fineness of spirit which alone can command the highest and finest work on the part of the incumbent. Right now the position of city manager, offering as it does an opportunity for reputation and honor on the part of the occupant, has this certain prospect of professional promotion "as its chiefest attribute and its chiefest incentive to able, ambitious administrators."

FRENCH CITY GOVERNMENT.—The professional idea is a basic one in France. The efficiency of the whole municipal fabric is bound up in the effectiveness with which the technically trained under-officials discharge their duties. The permanent professional executives of the departments, as, for example, *le secrétaire de maire,* chief of the clerical force of the city, are the backbone of the whole system.

Professor Munro says as to their body of professional administrators: "It would not be too much to say that the cities of France are administered very largely by corps of permanent municipal officials acting under a broad range of authority committed to them by the mayors. Though apparently vested in the hands of the layman, the administration is in reality, therefore, distinctly professional." The whole underlying fabric, then, of municipal government in French cities is founded upon this army of trained men who, by virtue of experience and technical training, master the details of public office, adjust the complicated machinery of officialdom, and create that record of efficiency commonly accredited solely to their laymen-superiors.

CHAPTER IV

THE POWER OF THE ELECTORATE

The lines upon which national parties divide have no necessary connection with the business of the city. Such connections open the way to countless schemes of public plunder and civic corruption.

THEODORE ROOSEVELT

The Divorce of the City and the National Party.—Parties have been treated as the chiefest elements in democratic government. And parties, it is true, are the vitals of politics, but "what we call politics," says Rt. Hon. James Bryce, "lies within the action of the nation and the national government," and not within the sphere of the city.

There is no more signal indication of the trend of popular action than the change in the powers of the electorate. We, as satisfied citizens of what we have assumed was a quite perfect democracy, have been wont to content ourselves with the cant phrases of "by" and "of" and "for the people." We have even prided ourselves on that shrewd, ingenious way in which we have devised checks and balances on the actions of officials to insure a fool-proof system of genuine honesty. We have even gone so far as to congratulate ourselves upon a complicated ballot, because we thought we could, forsooth, have the inestimable privilege of voting for each and every one of a number of miscellaneous officers, few of whom we knew personally and little of whose duties we ever comprehended. Intricacy and complication and a so-called political system had their glamour, but the hour of glamour as an excuse for inefficiency and indirection is no more.

A Dollar-for-Dollar Deal.—The people of the American city have taken in personal hand the workings of municipal government. They demand a dollar-for-dollar deal. To make sure of such treatment they must have the exclusive power to determine policies and to direct the administration of the city's affairs; and, once having gained the power, they must devise a means of retention of it.

That old system of checks and balances, while perhaps a thing of poetic beauty to the professional politician, has proved a disastrous failure in our city life. The customary blanket ballot with name after name in long and confusing arrangement headed at each column by a symbol of party allegiance for the guidance of the faithful, has proved a mighty instrument for the instructed, politically inclined few, but has been signally deficient as a means of expression of the real popular will. It were so much easier to put the cross-mark beneath the party symbol than to laboriously exercise the faculty of mind and select from the tedious array of names the man who should happen to be the fittest for the place for which he was candidate. "Let others think for you" is an easy doctrine indeed. As a consequence there was not much opposition to the party leader when he selected the candidates for his following to vote for. And the voter voted because the party had indorsed the candidate; the candidate ran because he was selected by the party leader; and the party leader selected him because he would be useful. Things work well in perfect circles of politics.

The Test.—The ultimate test, then, of fitness as a candidate was political affiliation. Yet the test when elected was that of efficient performance of the duties of the office. No wonder the job and the man seldom met and fitted at the City Hall. More often it was the method of selection rather than the official who was really to blame. And the conscientious officer who did feel the responsibilities of public service would often find,

> I have done some offense
> That seems disgracious in the city's eye,

without realizing that the cause was his own unpreparedness.

The Objective Point.—This was the condition in the average city. To secure the fabled benefits of life in a magic municipality administered by popular direction, it has been found that national and municipal politics must be divorced for, perforce, their issues and the qualifications of their candidates were alien. It was found that the ballot must be simplified so that the ordinary citizen could select with some facility men prominent enough to be well known as fitted for the duties of an office well understood. This was a step toward the elimination of selection by party leaders for political reasons and substituting efficiency as the test of choice. It was realized that means must be devised for the people to express their desires as to policies and plans at times other than the regular elections; that they must have means to negative policies contrary to popular will; that they might have means of remedying their mistakes of judgment in the selection of officials, at times other than the regularly constituted elections.

Means of Accomplishment

Short Ballot.—The short ballot is the new instrument placed in the hands of the electorate for the exercise of their power. This movement from out of the maze of popular indifference and away from the spirit of *laissez faire* has entailed the fall of many old political ideals. There is no more startling expression than this of the new spirit of the voters.

We have been weaned away from the former ideal of voting for a man for every possible office at every election. The moss-grown method of balancing one man's actions nicely against the evils another might do, and the venerable use of the party emblem at the head of the ballot, have both, in company with many other similar practices, met the fate of those who, well tried, have been found wanting in the crucial test of actual service. With this genesis of popular thought comes the new ballot having the few names of a few prominent men for worth-while offices, elected at intervals sufficiently apart to give them an opportunity to demonstrate what they can do in the way of service to the city as competent administrators. It gives the able man an opportunity to capitalize his ability for the benefit of the city.

"Political conditions are changed by the ideals of the people," said Senator Burton of Ohio, but it is still more true that the ideals of the people vary with political conditions. The political condition of inefficiency has largely shaken popular belief in the soundness of our city system. Persuaded to the need of change, remedial measures met a ready welcome. No longer the cumbersome, complicated, exasperatingly technical ballot sheet blanketing the will of the voter! No longer the party emblem as the ready password for the illiterate voter! The small and simple and sensible ballot has survived the carpings of the technical, the bugaboo of unconstitutionality and the vicious attacks of the reactionary. The gospel of efficiency, of simplicity and of directness, we may say, has had its effect.

This sterling principle has gained wide recognition. It is the true basis of city government and the city manager plan of government. It insists that first and foremost the voter must exercise his mind. It fulfills the demand that the voter must have the means to cast his vote intelligently. It is agreed that very few offices should be filled by election at one time. It is conceded that only those offices should be elective which are important enough to attract and hold public interest and inspection. These, then, are the crucial elements of success in the short ballot.

Wards Must Go.—The spirit of sectionalism has dominated the political life of every city. Ward pitted against ward, alderman against alderman, and legislation only effected by "log-rolling" extravagant measures into operation, mulcting the city, but gratifying the greed of constituents, has too long stung the conscience of decent citizenship. This constant treaty-making of factionalism has been no less than a curse. The city manager plan proposes the commendable thing of abolishing wards. The plan is not unique in this for it has been common to many forms of commission government, but it is mentioned here because the city manager plan is the embodiment of many of the virtues of experiments of the past in combination with certain original features of its own choosing. The abolition of wards is without doubt an innovation of profound value in cities under one hundred and fifty thousand population. In cities of this size and under the evils of ward systems were most apparent. The vicious system of patronage, of "log-rolling" and of selecting officials proposed by powerful aldermen for positions in the city government are all attendant evils upon treating the city, not as a unit, but as a conglomeration of disjointed and unrelated heterogeneous parts. By electing councilmen from wards and several at large, some wards were represented by two men, some by only one.

The new city is a unit. The new officers are elected each to represent all the people. Their duties are so defined that they must administer the corporate business in its entirety, not as a hodgepodge of associated localities. In large cities the wards are of such size that it would be impossible for a few men to be elected at large with any degree of success, for their knowledge of local conditions in various sections of the city would be very meager. The good in the retention of wards, therefore, in the larger cities is counterbalanced by the evil of selecting men at large, as above. It is suggested that it is better perhaps to permit a few large wards to each select a man or men well known and broad enough in their principles to regard their duty to the city as superior to their particular duty to any particular division of it or any group of constituents, and to abolish the election of numerous men from a ward or one man each from many wards. Those well versed in the retention of wards still consider it a matter of grave doubt whether it is advisable to retain them. This would be, however, a beneficial compromise.

The Initiative.—We have taken a grip on things.

It used to be a respectable political theory in the minds of those gentlemen who manipulated the ballot that once every so often, about election time, the public would probably have a sudden excess of unusual intelligence, that, upon the suggestion of these professional party leaders, wise in the ways of precincts and wards, the people would vote for the party man, and then the voters would lapse into a dignified apathy until the next voting period rolled around. Not so is the present attitude of the citizen. He prefers to dispense with the suggestion of the talented politician. He is determined to be master of his interest every day in the year and prefers not to delegate responsibility where he cannot exercise reasonable checks upon it. So long as he is called upon to pay every day for the acts of those he votes for, he ought to be allowed a proportionate amount of control. Paying every day should mean the privilege of voting every day, if that is the essential to the achievement of results.

The initiative is a method whereby a determined percentage of the voters can by petition present to the council or the commission a policy or plan for governmental adoption, and if refused, have it voted upon by the people at a duly constituted election. The basic idea is that the source of power is the people. This is, then, simply a means for

THE POWER OF THE ELECTORATE

permitting the people to exercise one of their own functions.

The details of carrying this idea into effect vary with the charters. In Dayton, Ohio, 10 per cent. of the total number of registered voters must sign the petition to propose an ordinance. If the commission rejects the proposed ordinance or passes it in a different form, the addition of 15 per cent., a total of 25 per cent., of such whole number of electors presents the matter for a general election and a vote by the people. In Springfield, Ohio, a city of about fifty thousand inhabitants, 5 per cent. of the electors may submit the ordinance, a public hearing before the commission to be had upon it, and, if rejected, or amended and then passed, 5 per cent. additional of the total number of registered voters can demand an election and a test of the question by a general vote upon the matter. The city of Springfield has also wisely provided that its legal officer, the city solicitor, shall draft the proposed ordinance so that it may be free from any legal defect and be embodied in proper approved legal form. These provisions are typical of similar proposals in other cities.

Referendum.—The partner of the initiative is the referendum. This is a provision in the city charter permitting the electorate, as a court of final appeal, to pass upon the measure itself and to adopt or reject it immediately, without waiting until a general election, when the only remedy would be the venting of popular displeasure upon the officials themselves by defeating them for reëlection. This makes it a question of policies immediately determined rather than a question of personalities of men distantly determined. It is a review and confirmation or rejection of a measure the legislative body has passed or refused to pass.

The details of the working of the broad principles of referendum are as various as the instruments adopted to carry them out. The charter of Springfield is typical of the provisions made for the citizens to keep check upon the performances of their representatives. It provides that no ordinance, unless it be an emergency measure, or an annual appropriation ordinance, shall go into effect until thirty days shall have elapsed after its passage. If within that time a petition bearing the names of 15 per cent. of the total number of registered voters is presented to the clerk of the city commission, requesting a repeal or an amendment, and the commission does not repeal or amend the ordinance, then, upon the request of a committee of petitioners, the question must be submitted to a vote of all the people. In Dayton the charter provides that the percentage of electors who must sign such a petition shall be twenty-five. These provisions are only one means of realizing the Jeffersonian ideal of power resident in and remaining with the electorate.

Recall.—A significant phrase occurs in Dayton's new charter: "Any or all of the Commissioners, or the City Manager, provided for in this Charter, may be removed from office by the electors."

This reminds us of that trite saying to the effect that a "wise man changes his mind, but a fool never considers this his privilege." The electorate for these many years voted at stated intervals and then lapsed into inaction, helpless at the hands of those they had helped and elevated to the powers of government. When those chosen few proved worthless or faithless in the course of the discharge of their trust, there was no remedy for a long-suffering public until the next elective period rolled around. There was no provision for the public to change its mind. The recall is in the nature of a prohibitory injunction on the inefficiency of public officials; the recall will enjoin the official by removing him from office and preventing any further display of his inefficiency, before an irreparable injury is done.

No business could be run on an office tenure of such a permanent kind as we used to endow our city with. The workings of the modern municipality have been found not to be alien at all to the management of great private industrial enterprises. It used to be the political fashion to be burdened with official incompetency from election to election, and then at these stated times to gather party forces and bring to bear keen persuasion to reëlect the burdensome gentleman because he was a faithful supporter of party principles and the obedient servant of political interests. The order of our present day has decreed otherwise. Elections can come frequently, necessitating the gathering of the organized hosts at too frequent intervals and entailing too expensive a program for the usual party organization to sustain. The strain is too great in many instances and the charges too large to whip into line always the organized ranks of the faithful. Elections come frequently then for the incompetent even though selected by a party and supported by a party; and it must be a strong man indeed to weather these cyclones of public disapproval.

The man who performs his duties faithfully, while open of course to being victimized by circumstances, will in the long run have little to fear from the changing whim of the people. The percentage of voters necessary for concentrated action is too great to allow the plan to become the instrument of a dissatisfied minority. It is objected that the official will be in constant fear of popular disfavor. Why not? The people elect him and they pay him and they suffer for his faults, so why should he not bear the burdens as well as the favors of the popular will? The American city official has so often held office for a period of years until his mind has become clouded with the illusion that he was gifted with the sovereign power of an eternal prerogative, and to insure official activity it is a good precept to teach that no lease on any public office is granted to any man.

Persuaded to this magic belief, then, that the people should at least be credited with moderate intelligence and granted the ultimate control of their own affairs, the city of Dayton provides that one-fourth of her registered voters may raise the question of recall by petition and if the official objected to does not resign, a general election to test the question whether he shall continue in office shall be held.

A very wise provision exists in most charters in providing a period of immunity for the official during which he may have an opportunity to make good. This period is usually six months in length during which he can demonstrate his abilities and capacity. In terms of office at least four years in length it would perhaps be well to extend the probationary period to a year. Furthermore, in order to prevent the office from becoming vacant, it is sometimes provided that a certain per cent. of the electors must nominate others to fill the position of the departing official before his recall will become complete.

The charter of Springfield includes a wise and just provision. It requires each recall petition briefly and succinctly to state the ground of complaint. The official is thus confronted with the charge fairly and squarely and all men who vote may read upon the face of the charge the nature of the indictment.

CONCLUSION

These city manager plans embrace, therefore, the progressive ideas of recent years. These ideas are adjuncts of the plan. How necessary to its operation, how vital to the successful working of the plan they may be, it is too early to venture a conclusive opinion. The cautious investigation of experts results in the recommendation of these features as fundamental elements in its successful operation.

CHAPTER V

THE NEW COMMISSION

For policy one must elect, and for efficiency one **must** appoint.
CLINTON ROGERS WOODRUFF

Happily, the idea of a business corporation is largely synonymous with efficiency, in the minds of the American people. The design of running a city in the same excellent way was received with profound satisfaction. It appealed to the genius and the talents of the electorate. When the reformers talked of "boards of directors" and "managers" and "auditing systems," they were conversing in language that needed no explanation. Their hearers were already experts in the subject.

The selection of the analogy was thus a fortuitous one. When a commission was proposed to administer city affairs like a board of a private corporation, the idea met with vigorous approval for it tickled the fancy of the citizen. So the commission form of government was born with a cognomen that predisposed the popular mind to its adoption, even if the circumstances of the great disaster in Galveston had not initially started it well on its successful way.

The Error.—The idea of commission government was basically good. Yet in practice it was never carried far enough to enrich the people with the full meed of results they should have had. As to an advisory or legislative board the idea was economically and politically sound. The attempt has been made, however, in all forms practically, except the city manager plan, to combine in the commission both legislative and executive functions. This was an error. The old system of checks and balances of the federal plan was good in itself; only, the application was a blunder. When the commission had combined in itself both legislative and executive powers the advantages of the checks of one division of government on the other were lost.

Remedy in the City Manager Plan.—The plan of placing an executive expert in charge of the administration of the municipality eliminates this single objection. The commission retains its legislative function, its advisory capacity, its power to formulate broadminded policies and wise plans. Vital also is the fact that where the personnel of the commission is not required to devote all its time to the details of administrative labor, in which such members of the commission generally have little previous experience, a widely different type of man is secured as a commissioner. An able, clear-sighted, successful business man would consent to act as a member of a commission purely legislative and advisory, whereas he must perforce decline to sacrifice his business by giving his whole time to so unlucrative a pursuit as the administration of a fractional part of a city government demanding all of his time. Then too his commendable qualities should not be taken from the business life of the city where they are already radically good in his position as a progressive citizen. His capacity and experience should be utilized without hampering his business productiveness and its consequent benefit to the community.

The city manager plan recognizes and meets this impediment to success. It places the commissioner in a position which his previous business experience has fitted him for, namely, advice on business problems. The execution is left to an expert who is highly trained in that field of endeavor and wholly competent to cope with it. The spheres of action of the advisor and administrator are wholly distinct and separate.

Charter Provisions.—The system of elections under the new charters usually provides for a primary election for commissioners. They are nominated by petitions signed by a certain per cent. of the unregistered voters of the municipality. In Dayton it is 2 per cent. Those candidates receiving the highest number of votes, in a number double the size of the commission, are placed on the final ballot without designation of party or presence of distinguishing emblem. It is simply a question of the candidate himself. Where the ballots are made up in tablet form, the names of the candidates are rotated so that there is no advantage of one man over another.

Abolition of Wards.—All ward lines are abolished and the election is generally at large. In Hickory, North Carolina, in its recent charter, a provision is made for nomination from wards, but the election is at large. In La Grande, Oregon, preferential voting is provided with the usual first, second and third choices. Phœnix, Arizona, provides for one election, nomination by primary, and a second election if necessary to secure a majority vote to fill one or more vacancies.

Qualifications of Commissioners.—The prerequisites for election as a commissioner are as varied as the number of charters. Springfield requires five years' residence and the qualifications of an elector; Dayton provides no time limit of residence, but specifically forbids any interest of the commissioner in public contracts, thus wisely enforcing the Biblical maxim that service to one master is all one man can successfully render. Favors, free tickets, passes or service, direct or indirect from corporations, persons or firms upon terms more advantageous to the recipient than those generally accorded to the public are universally forbidden to the commissioner. The commissioner is set apart from influences of gain, fear or favor. Springfield forbids personal solicitation of names by the candidate, for his petition of candidacy; only the channels of public address and the public press are open to him to declare his beliefs and policies, and he is to be known and elected by these declarations alone. Surely the old order is changing. The proposed Lockport plan defines the qualifications of the alderman or commissioner to "be the highest non-professional or non-technical qualifications specified for any officer under the charter."

Term of Office.—The term of office varies in the several cities. In La Grande, Oregon, the period of incumbency is one year; in Hickory, North Carolina, two years; while in Dayton and Springfield it is four years. The latter term is preferable for otherwise no policy ever formulated can be carried to maturity and completely tested by those who inaugurated it. This was the defect in the old government, the constant vacillation from policy to policy, from hobby to hobby, as new mayor succeeded new mayor, and new councilman followed new councilman. In nearly all these charters provision is made for election at periods during the total time of office tenure so that new men are constantly being made members without a wholesale change of personnel of the body. For instance, in Dayton, there is an election every two years for two men for four years of service and every other two years for three men for four years of office.

Mayor.—In the last-named city, in the election at which the places of three members in its commission are filled, the candidate receiving the highest number of votes is declared mayor. To extend the simile of modern business organization, the mayor in a city under the commissioner manager form of government is chairman or president of the board of directors, or chairman of the executive committee. He is still the official head of the government with retention, in many cases, of his power in case of riot or other disaster, to command the police force and govern by proclamation; he is still recognized head of the government for service of civil process by the courts and respected by the citizens as head of the municipality for ceremonial purposes.

The mayor is now shorn of his veto power. He has a vote and voice in the acts and proceedings of the commission, but his old potency as a separate factor in legislation with power to block at will much that was enacted, has been taken from him. As a presiding officer, the new mayor is chosen for his sagacity and good judgment and business ability; he is not chosen as an administrator, nor as one to act in a judicial capacity, nor as a political figurehead, nor as a man with an attractive hobby to ride at the expense of the city.

The question will sometimes arise, what is the proper procedure when a mayor is recalled. In the Dayton charter it is provided, that the commissioners shall select one of the remaining number as mayor, or, if all commissioners are recalled, then, of the newly elected commissioners, the one receiving the highest vote shall be adjudged mayor.

Salaries.—There has been a general readjustment in salaries paid the city officials. The compensation paid the mayor of Dayton is $1,800 per annum, and each of the commissioners receives $1,200. In connection with this provision, Dayton makes this peculiar reservation: that absence of any commissioner from a regular meeting of a commission,

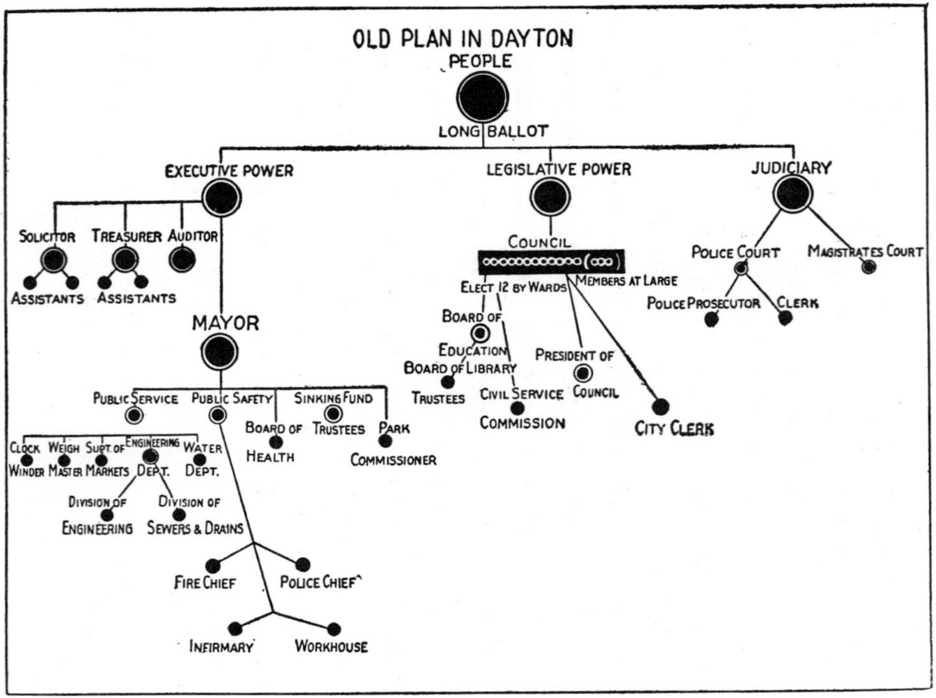
OLD PLAN IN DAYTON
PEOPLE
LONG BALLOT
EXECUTIVE POWER
LEGISLATIVE POWER
JUDICIARY
SOLICITOR
TREASURER
AUDITOR
ASSISTANTS
ASSISTANTS
MAYOR
COUNCIL
ELECT 12 BY WARDS
MEMBERS AT LARGE
BOARD OF EDUCATION
BOARD OF LIBRARY TRUSTEES
CIVIL SERVICE COMMISSION
PRESIDENT OF COUNCIL
CITY CLERK
POLICE COURT
MAGISTRATES COURT
POLICE PROSECUTOR
CLERK
PUBLIC SERVICE
PUBLIC SAFETY
SINKING FUND TRUSTEES
BOARD OF HEALTH
PARK COMMISSIONER
CLOCK WINDER
WEIGH MASTER
SUPT. OF MARKETS
ENGINEERING DEPT.
WATER DEPT.
DIVISION OF ENGINEERING
DIVISION OF SEWERS & DRAINS
FIRE CHIEF
POLICE CHIEF
INFIRMARY
WORKHOUSE

unless authorized by a majority vote of that body, shall automatically cause a reduction of 1 per cent. of the annual salary; and absence, unauthorized by the commission, for five consecutive meetings "operates to vacate the seat of a member." It is evidently intended that a man must attend to business in this city of newer ideals. Similar provisos and penalties are found in other charters under the city manager plan. Likewise, there is often a specification that the meetings must occur not less than a stated number of times per year.

Division of Powers.—The scope of powers accorded to the new commission is distinctly referable to late experiences with these newer forms of government. It is a return to the division of powers, devolving the legislative responsibilities upon a board and the administrative upon an individual. The combination of the two functions in one organization is inimical to the best that can be had from the ideas behind the promotion of the modern municipalities. Our national tradition of separation of the two powers has not proved the fallacious theory reformers would have had us believe.

Publicity.—A very wise precaution is that which provides that all meetings of this commission are to be public and that the people are to have access to all the minutes and records detailing their proceedings. This has been found to be an essential right in private corporations, and the citizen is no less than a stockholder in the public corporation. These advanced charters are more and more looking to this fundamental requirement of publicity; but before we can have the results these provisions contemplate, the chiefest requirement will be to make these records understandable by the ordinary person without expert knowledge. Provisions are embodied in many places in these instruments under which the newer governments operate, which have this end in contemplation, providing for simpler accounts, simpler auditing systems, publication of readable reports, condensed, epitomized, and analyzed for the rapid and intelligent understanding by the voters of the acts of the governing officials. Municipal bureaus of research have done much toward giving this required publicity and coöperation, and toward promoting intelligent, reliable publication of essential pieces of civic information. They have been marvelous factors for the education of the citizen body for the comprehensive understanding of puzzling difficulties. As an instance of this, the Dayton bureau has been a typical case of the virtues of such an organization.

Public Hearings.—It is set forth in the provisions for enactment of the appropriation ordinance, in

Dayton's charter, that a time and place shall be fixed for public hearings on the tentative ordinance, and that public notice shall be given of the hearings. After the public hearing, but before the commission passes the ordinance, it is to be published in parallel with the recommendation of the city manager. The ordinance cannot be passed till ten days shall have elapsed after its publication, and never before the second Monday in January. Expert advice, public opinion and discussion, and time for sober thought will all enter in their proportionate parts into the final enactment of a sound financial program for the year. It is a measure fraught with advantage for government and people. The government officials cannot be blamed for not taking the people into their confidence; and it places the burden of knowing the situation on those most vitally concerned, namely, the taxpayers. This appropriation is final and money cannot be drawn before the hearing, or any obligation entered into for an expenditure except in accordance with this fiscal method. The commission has power, however, upon recommendation of the city manager, to apply unexpended balances, after an object has been accomplished, to the completion of objects also contemplated, but lacking enough funds to consummate them.

Springfield has provided the excellent scheme of

the publication of ordinances of a permanent or general nature once within ten days after final passage. Special form for general notice of public improvements is also provided in addition to notice to be served on interested property holders.

Powers of Commission.—Under the commission manager form of government two distinct powers are accorded the commissioners: first, a limited appointive power, and, second, legislative power. The appointive power is vested in them because the proposed personnel of the commission is such that it is capable of selecting the major executive, and this power is limited because it should be left to the major executive himself to select those for whose work and efficiency he will be responsible. The commissioners are granted power to pass ordinances, for thus they can promulgate in tangible form the policies they may, in the light of their experience, determine upon; in ordinances they can embody the plans and measures the city manager may propose to them in his advisory capacity, which they shall deem expedient.

Appointive Power.—The duty of selection of the city manager rests upon the commission. They find him, determine the salary according to the man, and appoint him to the position. There is no ratification, except a negative sort which may be

THE NEW COMMISSION

evidenced by the electorate in recalling the commission or the city manager. In Springfield, the commission appoints the city manager, the city solicitor, city auditor, city treasurer, purchasing agent, sinking fund commissioner, and civil service commissioner. In Dayton, the commission appoints the city manager, civil service board, and the clerk of the commission. In Hickory, North Carolina, the council appoints the city manager, city attorney, city treasurer, city physician, the board of school visitors, superintendent of schools, and the judge of the municipal court. In the last-named city, the local judiciary and educational system are identified with the city government. In towns of any size this is a provision of very doubtful wisdom. The judiciary should be conspicuously independent of current municipal problems, and should be so individual as to be outside of politics as far as possible, yet constantly subject to the independent, searching scrutiny of the public whom it serves. The municipal judiciary systems are problems in themselves. In Hickory, also, certain subordinate officers are appointed by the council from lists submitted by the city manager for the police, fire, street, waterworks and sewerage departments; and officers are appointed to positions in the health department from a list submitted by the city physician and in the school department from a list supplied by the superintendent of schools. There are no civil service provisions in that city.

In La Grande, Oregon, the general manager and municipal judge are appointed by the commission of three members. There are no civil service provisions. In Phœnix, Arizona, the commission appoints the city manager, the city magistrate and city auditor, unrestricted by civil service requirements.

Miscellaneous Boards: Civil Service.—The civil service board stood alone in all former governments as the sole attempt to introduce efficiency. In the old governments this was well enough as far as it went, but it only provided for the prerequisite of efficiency to secure the job, and provided nothing for continued efficiency in the same position; and arranged nothing looking to the gradation of a salary according to the amount of labor the position entailed, the amount of training preliminary to the successful discharge of its duties; nor was there ever required to be kept a record of the subsequent conduct of the successful candidate in actual performance of duty, after his final qualification resultant from a probationary period during the first few months of service. It is human to let down in activity after the first blush of newness and when ambition wears off and the occupant of the position falls into a rut. In private commercial life to hold your place in a business organization, eternal efficiency is the price of place. This fundamental maxim seldom seems to have appealed to the city governments. Even when political considerations were somewhat swept aside by the meritorious civil service provisions, yet nothing was substantially provided to secure for the future continued adequate zeal of officials, which is most important of all. Many men can qualify under the spur, but real efficiency records are writ despite the daily grind of current monotonous events.

Equal Pay for Equal Work.—In this latest of charters adopted by the city of Dayton, it is proposed to give equal pay for equal work. This may seem a strange thing for a progressive city to be just waking up to; nevertheless, under the old government, an assistant solicitor with professional training received $2,000 per annum, while a record clerk, with no large amount of preliminary preparation and only meager work, drew the same salary. That was a triple injustice: injustice first to the other employees, injustice to the city which did not get what it was paying for, and injustice to the long-suffering taxpayer. To take the new civil service board of Dayton as typical, it is to be composed of three members of six years' tenure, one appointed every two years by the commission. Any member of the board may be removed by the commission upon written reasons being presented and a hearing afforded in defense; vacancies are filled by the same body. The civil service board elects its own chairman from its number; selects its secretary, who is the chief examiner and the employment officer for the classified service of the city; and appoints such other subordinates as an appropriation is made for.

Rules.—The board enacts its code of rules, to be approved by the commission. This code has for its object the appointment of officials upon a basis of merit, efficiency, character and industry, which rules have all the effect of law. Promotion in the classified service is provided by the board to be made as the records of merit, efficiency, character, conduct and seniority may justify. The word "records" marks a signal departure in charter framing. At last we are entered upon an era of proof of proficiency, rather than proof of political affiliation. The probationary period of six months is still present. No discharge or removal of a department head or city manager is final until the aggrieved shall be heard by the board in his own defense in response to written, specific charges. This new government is setting out to have short-handed justice too. Before an official can be paid as a member of the force rightfully appearing on the payroll, the payroll must be certified to by the board; a wise check indeed.

Standards.—Furthermore, the employees covered by civil service rules are forbidden to display any political activity; but no discrimination is to be made because of religious belief, race, or political affiliation. The board determines the penalties for the violation of this rule.

Compensation.—The commission is to determine and appropriate the salaries of members of the board and the subordinates, providing at the same time a sum adequate to secure the operation of the provision. In this connection, it is to be remarked that the commission fixes by ordinance the compensation of department heads, of the city manager, the compensation of the members of the police and fire force who are under the immediate control of the chief, of the members of boards in the unclassified service of the city. The salaries will be uniform.

In the matter of boards there should be mentioned the trustees of the sinking fund. In Dayton it is provided that the commissioners, city manager, and director of finance shall constitute the trustees, the mayor being president and the director the secretary.

Springfield provides that the members of its civil service board shall serve without pecuniary compensation. In the matter of boards, it also provides that additional ones may be constituted by the commission to advise the commission, the manager, or heads of the departments with respect to the conduct and management of any property, institution or public function of the city. The members of such consulting boards are to serve without compensation. This plan has the sterling recommendation in that it enlists intimately the active service of the leading citizens, calling upon them to contribute their share in special cases for which their abilities peculiarly adapt them. The closer the citizen is to the management of his city, the better the city. It is the age-old problem of keeping up the interest of the electorate.

Power of Commission: Legislation.—The commission has a second general power, that of legislation. It may pass ordinances granting franchises which, like all measures it may enact, shall be subject to the initiative and referendum. This principle has one exception in the case of emergency measures. A franchise ordinance, however, is not considered an emergency measure. The city is at liberty to terminate a franchise at will upon specified terms or to purchase the utility, yet no ordinance is valid unless the value of the franchise is excluded from the purchase valuation of the property.

Scope of Ordinances.—Appropriations are enforced and salaries determined by ordinance. The commission, in one city, may at any time borrow money or authorize the issuance of notes or bonds therefor in anticipation of the collection of assessments, levied for the purpose of paying the cost of certain public improvements. The commission customarily establishes rules of bidding for public contracts. Ordinances may furthermore be submitted to the commission by initiative and passed, amended, or rejected as they see fit. Even emergency ordinances are subject to referendum, except that they go into immediate effect and continue in operation until rejected by the voters, but the ordinance is authority for all things done in pursuance of it prior to its rejection. The commission may also order proper investigations of the acts of any official and it has power to subpœna witnesses, hear testimony, and compel production of books for pertinent purposes.

Advisory Boards.—It is the spirit of our times to employ commissions, committees, or boards to investigate; it is the temper of the public to employ specialists for unconventional jobs.

A municipal administration needs such a body of men to assist, and it needs experts. To secure the proper personnel as a permanent feature was too costly. A happy compromise has been employed in the commission manager plan. A board of experts is selected and asked to serve in an advisory capacity for a restricted particular purpose. The specialists are thus secured and complimented, and serve without the onerous burden of extensive duties, to their own and the city's benefit.

Springfield provides:

"The city commission at any time may appoint an advisory board or boards composed of citizens qualified to act in an advisory capacity to the city commission, the city manager or the head of any department, with respect to the conduct and management of any property, institution or public function of the city. The members of any such board shall serve without compensation for a time fixed in their appointment, or at the pleasure of the commission; and their duty shall be to consult and advise with such municipal officers and make written recommendations which shall become part of the records of the city."

Dayton provides:

"The Commission may appoint a City Plan Board and upon the request of the City Manager shall appoint advisory boards. The members of such boards shall serve without compensation and their duty shall be to consult and advise with the various departments. The duties and powers thus created shall be prescribed by ordinance."

These provisions permit the appointment of the city's best talent, and perhaps even outside persons of skill in the particular field the board is appointed to investigate. City plan boards, commissions to investigate the accounting system or the water system, river and harbor experts, and building code specialists, are a few of the many types of men from which such advisory boards are to be recruited. English and German, as well as the French, city governments have long realized the value of commissions and committees to administer civic affairs; while not of the exact type of the present boards in question, yet in many cases unpaid civilian members, as in Germany, have been used on boards to administer particular departments or municipal ventures in some special field. It is a commendable practice which should be extensively developed.

Trustees of Public Trusts.—The commissioners are the trustees of the public trust: they are the connecting links between the people and the manager. As a board of legislators, they mold the policy of the administration; as a board of direction, they appoint and select the agency of execution. The commission is the balance wheel of the machinery of government, acting as a check on the one hand on the facile popular will and on the other hand acting as a restraining and guiding agency in the affairs of the city manager. The powers of this new commission are not diminished in importance as compared with what they were in other commission governments, but merely adjusted more nicely to the delicate requirements of municipal administration.

CHAPTER VI

THE CITY MANAGER

The ingenuity of each generation has developed quicker and better methods for doing every element of the work in every trade.   Frederick Winslow Taylor

The Old School.—Municipal management is an arduous art. There is no other species of business specialty which duplicates it for the requirements of sagacity and tact and constructive leadership. No variety of industrial organization is fraught with more difficulties of economy, of efficiency, of absolute control imposed upon one competent man. Yet for decades we have flouted the idea that the public corporation is different from other businesses. We blithely assumed that the average city official, selected on the basis of political influence, was endowed with God-given faculties of administrative ability. We calmly assumed that private corporations and public corporations were different on the business side and yet we have straightway put into office men who, at best, had had experience with only one form of corporation. We thought that a group of men of no particularly tested fitness, allowed a short period of power, with no well-defined policy, or, at all events, merely a hobby, could run a many-million dollar corporation with the triple aspect of a business and a human and a governmental side. We paid small salaries to men of minute experience with conflicting interests and tempting opportunities for enriching themselves at public expense. And then we wondered where our taxes went and why results did not come in the fabled way of Aladdin's Lamp.

Tradition shackles genuine advance. It has been tradition for the cities to be wasteful; it has been tradition for them to be inefficient and then to blame the vicious result upon corrupt practices; it has been tradition to pay for a great deal we never received and to suffer for the carelessness we voted for others to commit. Tradition scorned the idea of an executive specially trained in the technical work of civic administration.

Lately the citizens have stood at the gateway of a new day. It was either a break with the ancient forms or a continued living with tradition and old ideals and bankruptcy. Many are choosing the former.

Promulgation of commission government was fine work in the rearrangement of the old units of gov-

CITY MANAGER PLAN, DAYTON, OHIO.

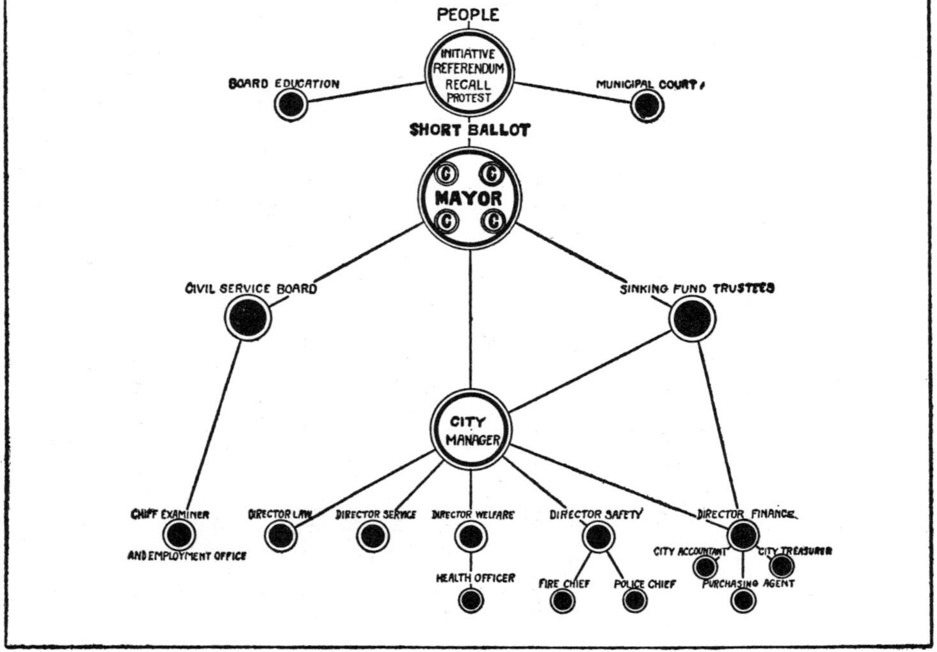

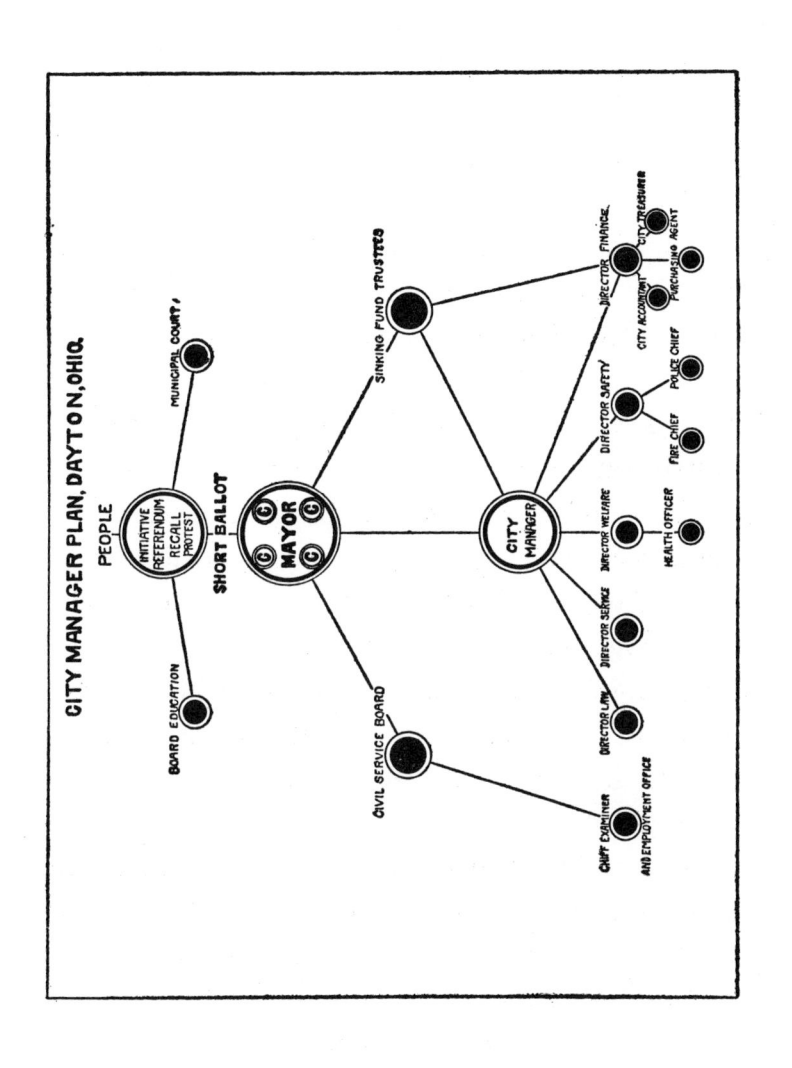

ernment. Creation of the office of city manager was a genuine departure into an unexplored realm of administration. In the designation of a city manager there was proposed a new officer with original duties and fresh powers. What a tempting problem in constructive politics!

The City Manager.—The city manager is an appointive officer selected, by reason of his peculiar knowledge of municipal affairs and because of his administrative ability, to fill the position of chief executive of a vast public corporation, with little restriction upon his power and with only one command—produce results. He has been defined as "a competent, experienced, trained and capable person selected on account of his peculiar fitness and ability to manage the affairs of the city."

Qualifications.—Municipal managership is a new profession. As the requirements of the office are largely untried, the charter framers displayed keen foresightedness in making the qualifications for service of broad general character without regard to hampering details. Theirs was the intent to secure the best man at a price which would be justified by the results he would produce. These provisions as to his qualifications are so general and so liberal in their tendencies that the restrictions take on merely a negative character. For instance,

THE CITY MANAGER

the charters generally state that the city manager need not be selected from citizens resident in the city, but may be appointed from any locality, as it is a question of ability rather than residence.

Dr. Washington Gladden at the Conference of Ohio Cities in 1912 said:

"Still another shackle would be broken if our new constitution should remove all those limitations by which the people are restricted, in selecting their officials, to residents of their own city. Why should not the city corporation be free in choosing its employees—to take them wherever it can find them—to get the best men without any reference to their place of residence? No business corporation would submit to such a restriction, that it should employ in an executive capacity none but its own stockholders or none but residents in its own community. Cases often arise in which far more efficient service might be secured by going outside of the municipality. For special services we sometimes do go outside; but why should we limit ourselves at all? It is sometimes assumed that a resident of the neighborhood would know the people better, and would then be able to serve them more acceptably; but the fact is that, as a rule, the less people a municipal officer knows, the better it is for the service. The great curse of municipal government arises from the fact that the officials know too many people, and are under too many obligations. It will take a competent executive but a very short time to get all the knowledge of local conditions that will be of any use to him."

His personal qualifications above all are essential. His political beliefs are especially mentioned as a thing which shall not be considered a bar in any way whatsoever to his candidacy. The test of politics is a dead letter; the measurement of efficiency is a live issue.

So much for the general, though meager, qualifications so briefly enumerated by the charters. They are chiefly concerned with what he is not to be. The unspoken qualifications, undoubtedly the chiefest in the make-up of a man in such a position are, first, absolute, unswerving adherence to his own view that efficiency, and hence results for the city, is the paramount thing; second, administrative experience in business involving the maintenance of engineering works and the necessary technical education; and third, the ability to lead through tact as well as knowledge.

The New Profession's Personnel.—The city managers selected for Staunton, Sumter, Springfield and Dayton have preëminently these qualities. The selections in each case by the commissions have been the result of patient search and careful thought and profound study of what were the requirements of the position and qualities which one should have to adequately fill it.

The first city managers of Dayton and Springfield are illustrative of the type of men required for the position. Mr. H. M. Waite was appointed city manager of Dayton. He is a civil engineer by profession, graduating from the Massachusetts Institute of Technology. He has been superintendent of maintenance of way and superintendent of various divisions of the large railways of this country. He made a remarkable record as city engineer for the city of Cincinnati. In that position he distinguished himself for efficiency of administration, a knowledge of civic affairs and an absolute unswerving loyalty to the idea of efficiency in public office. Equipped with a profound sense of the importance of public service, he chose his subordinates with an eye to their ability to serve the people rather than a political machine; he was subservient to no party and to the dictates of no ascendant political organization. At the time of his assumption of office on January 1, 1914, in the city of Dayton, he was forty-three years of age, a man of wide technical and administrative experience, possessing a record of efficient service under that advanced administration in the city of Cincinnati in the late régime of Mayor Hunt. A most telling indication of his policies was his first statement upon the assumption of power in his new position. "I insist," he said, "when I employ men for work in my department that they be selected for their efficiency and not because of any political affiliation or in payment of any political debts, and this same policy I expect to adhere to in Dayton." That is a platform well worth while indeed.

The city manager of Springfield is another man with a record of most excellent service. Mr. Charles E. Ashburner, also aged forty-three, lately of Lynchburg, Virginia, was selected first city manager for the city of Springfield. He is a native of England, the son of an officer in the English army. After an excellent education in Germany and France he came to America and found his first employment as civil engineer in the Rivers and Harbors Bureau of the United States. Later, he was engaged by a contracting firm on engineering projects in various countries of the world and then was employed by a railway in its engineering department. His first municipal experience was in Staunton, Virginia, where he became city manager, when the general manager was installed there. He was therefore probably the first city manager in America; furthermore, he installed the excellent city manager system now in force in Sumter, North Carolina. After that, he went back to his profession from which he was called lately to assume the place of chief executive of this city of fifty thousand.

When the commission selects the city manager, it is a part of its power to fix his salary. The spirit of the charters in the larger cities, as in Springfield and Dayton, is to have the best at any price. The commissioners are at liberty to bargain with a prospective candidate in regard to the place and to secure the best man their finances will justify, according to the customary method in the business world.

To the uninitiated sometimes the salary of a city manager looks high. It is, and in this matter of high salaries lies a grave danger for the success of the plan. A large salary can only be justified when its recipient saves the city the excess and more by his economy of administration without impairment of results. A high salary is economy when it purchases ability which enables the public corporation not only to pay the man, but to secure results and produce a profit instead of the usual yearly deficit. It is not a matter of extravagance or erroneous business policy to pay the head of a private corporation, numbering its assets in the millions, an excellent salary. No more should it be unsound policy to pay well a man who administers a public corporation of like tangible value, and of far more import to the citizens, who are stockholders in it in a thousand intangible ways. For the very life of the citizenry itself is bound up in the sane determination of the city's affairs. It is a vital fact of existence itself which demands that we should pay the price, if we only secure that efficiency which means health and protection and the opportunity to produce as we should. Both business and social reasons proclaim it a wise thing indeed to pay well a competent man who will make these things possible. Believing this to be true, the little city of Staunton pays her manager $2,500 per annum; Sumter pays $3,300; Springfield pays $6,000; and Dayton pays $12,500. These are goodly annual sums, but if the theory of the new government upon which these salaries are paid is carried out, there will be ample justification in the resulting economy.

The selection of the manager devolves solely on the commission. It is a very vital task and one of profound moment to the people. It is of telling importance to the commissioners themselves, for their success as a body depends largely upon the qualities which the man they select possesses. It behooves them to weigh with exceeding care this, the chiefest officer in the municipality, and to cull out from those proposed for the office all the ineligible, and to secure the fittest remaining. It is true that they are at liberty to remove him at will, but this may not always be a practical power and may not always be exercised in time to prevent the fruition of his wrongful acts. Theirs is the option either to let him alone so long as he conducts the affairs of his office satisfactorily to the people and to the commission or they must completely remove him from office. They do not have the privilege of retaining him in office and directing the methods that he may pursue for the achievement of results. Further than this, of course, the city manager is always subject to recall directly by the people. This affords the commission a peculiar advantage. In case affairs are not conducted properly, and it is apparently the fault of execution, and not the fault of legislation, then the commission, who are solely responsible for the inauguration of policies and plans, are exonerated from blame, and the people can vent their wrath upon the city manager alone if they so desire.

Powers.—Unique are the powers of the city manager. In him are concentrated all functions of appointment, of control of employees and of advice to the commission. In the Dayton and Springfield plan the power is so extensive, particularly in the former city, that the term "controlled-executive" is hardly applicable any more.

One thing is evident. His methods of achieving results are uncontrolled. The end, not the means, is the objective in these modern instruments of government. The powers and duties of the chief executive of the modern American city are, therefore, quite unprecedented.

The charter of Springfield enumerates succinctly his powers in the following manner:

"(a) To see that the laws and ordinances are enforced.

"(b) Except as herein provided, to appoint and remove all heads of departments, and all subordinate officers and employees of the city; all appointments to be upon merit and fitness alone, and in the classified service all appointments and removals to be subject to the civil service provisions of this charter.

"(c) To exercise control over all departments and divisions created herein or that hereafter may be created by the commission.

"(d) To see that all terms and conditions imposed in favor of the city or its inhabitants in any public utility franchise are faithfully kept and performed; and upon knowledge of any violation thereof to call the same to the attention of the city solicitor, who is hereby required to take such steps as are necessary to enforce the same.

"(e) To attend all meetings of the commission, with the right to take part in the discussions but having no vote.

"(f) To recommend to the commission for adoption such measures as he may deem necessary or expedient.

"(g) To act as budget commissioner and to keep the city commission fully advised as to the financial condition and needs of the city; and

"(h) To perform such other duties as may be prescribed by this charter or be required of him by ordinance or resolution of the commission."

The city manager in this city is also empowered to act as the platting commissioner. This is of particular import in these days when it is very advisable to have a uniform method and plan of arranging the city. City platting has become a science in itself and should be administered by an expert who has a wide knowledge of the needs of the city, its urgent demands and the possibilities for the future.

Dayton empowers her city manager in the following manner:

"(a) To see that the laws and ordinances are enforced.

"(b) To appoint and, except as herein provided, remove all directors of departments and all subordinate officers and employees in the departments in both the classified and unclassified service; all appointments to be upon merit and fitness alone, and in the classified service all appointments and removals to be subject to the civil service provisions of this charter;

"(c) To exercise control over all departments and divisions created herein or that may be hereafter created by the Commission;

"(d) To attend all meetings of the Commission with the right to take part in the discussion but having no vote;

"(e) To recommend to the Commission for adoption such measures as he may deem necessary or expedient;

"(f) To keep the Commission fully advised as to the financial condition and needs of the city; and

"(g) To perform such other duties as may be prescribed by this charter or be required of him by ordinance or resolution of the Commission."

As exact knowledge of conditions in the departments and among employees is one of the requirements or one of the basic ideas in the new city government, it is quite in keeping to direct that the city manager may without notice cause an extensive investigation into the affairs of any of the departments under his control or the conduct of any officer or employee. This power of the manager to investigate is coupled with the power to compel the attendance of witnesses and the production of books and to punish for contempt in order to enforce the carrying out of his orders made in such manner.

In Hickory, North Carolina, the charter sets forth the powers of the city manager, not in an orderly or systematic fashion as in the well-drawn charters of the larger cities, but in an equally effective way. The powers it enumerates are about as follows:

(a) He shall attend all meetings of the council and make recommendations thereto and furnish information to it as may seem necessary within the wisdom of council or manager.

(b) He shall require an accurate report from those beneath him in various departments as to the performance of their duties.

(c) He shall sign all contracts, licenses and other documents on behalf of the city.

(d) He has the power of investigation.

(e) He has the power of revocation of licenses pending action of the city council.

(f) He has power over public works and build-

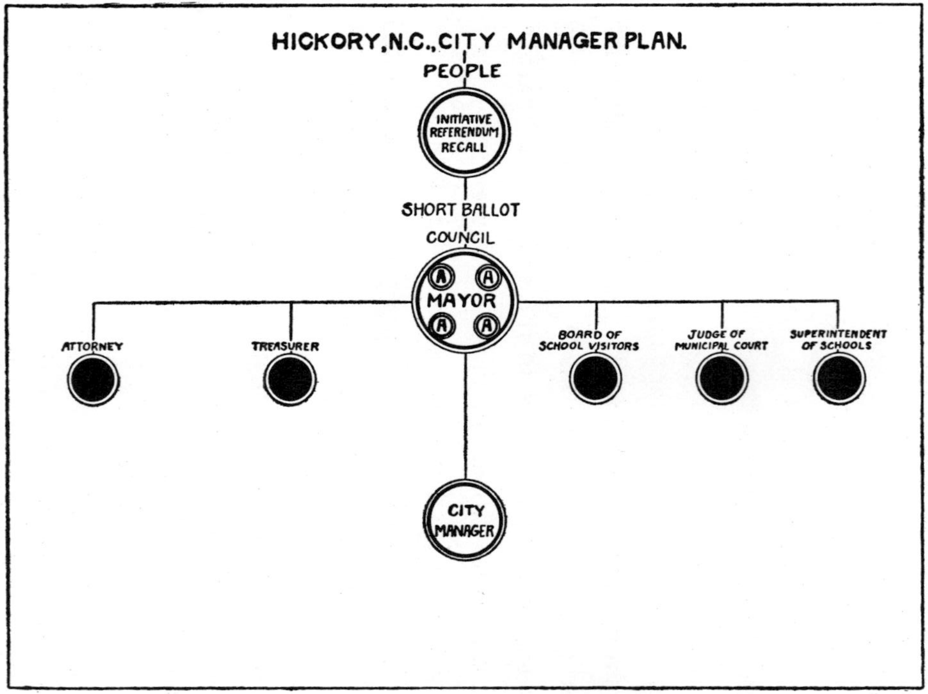
HICKORY, N.C., CITY MANAGER PLAN.
PEOPLE
INITIATIVE REFERENDUM RECALL
SHORT BALLOT
COUNCIL
A
A
MAYOR
A
A
ATTORNEY
TREASURER
BOARD OF SCHOOL VISITORS
JUDGE OF MUNICIPAL COURT
SUPERINTENDENT OF SCHOOLS
CITY MANAGER

ings, construction of public improvements, as highways, bridges, etc.; he has control of public utilities, whether publicly or privately owned; and he has charge of all the water supply and sewerage systems.

(g) He has power to suspend, fine or dismiss members of the police, fire, waterworks, sewerage and street departments in the interests of discipline.

(h) He shall submit a list to the city council from which are to be appointed for the term of one year the officers and employees of the police, fire, street, water and sewerage departments.

In La Grande, Oregon, the provision as to the power of the city manager is a very general one and consequently a very excellent one. In this city the general manager, so called, has absolute control and supervision over every office and the employees therein, except the commissioners and the municipal judge, and has the power of appointment of all other officers. He has the power to discharge his appointees with or without cause. He is to see that the business of the corporation is transacted "in a modern, scientific and business-like manner." He is to keep records like those kept by a private corporation. He is accountable to the commission for results.

From an analysis of the foregoing respective charters in the matter of powers given the city manager, the following are apparently the general powers usually conferred upon that official:

(a) He is charged with the enforcement of laws and ordinances.

(b) He administers the affairs of the departments and is responsible for the results obtained therefrom.

(c) He appoints and dismisses the employees whose work will produce the results he is responsible for.

(d) He advises the council and attends the meetings for that purpose, supplementing his advice with formal written reports, but he has no vote.

(e) He estimates the financial needs of the corporation and acting as expert budget maker he is financial adviser of the commission.

(f) He has the general powers of investigation and is the general agent of the commission.

Control of Salaries.—In the discussion of the departments, many of the limitations to the authority of the city manager have been already considered, but there are a number of miscellaneous powers untouched upon. In city government, no less than in war, a control over the payroll of the active participants, as the officers, is a potent thing. With the exception of department heads, direct employees of the commission, police and fire force, and board members in the unclassified service, all the vast number of remaining employees and officers have their compensation fixed virtually by the city manager. This is true of one charter at least, that of Dayton. And in this instrument it is still further wisely provided that uniform salaries shall be paid for like services, as such services shall be graded by the city manager in harmony with the civil service rules. Upon being so fixed, a report is made to the city employment officer of the size of salary for the particular office. In fixing the limit of these salaries the amount of the bond which the particular officer may be called upon to give for the faithful and honest performance of his duties is also determined by the city manager.

Financial Control.—The city manager should properly be in intimate relationship with the curtailment of expenditures. He should be in daily contact with the sources of income and outgo, for he is the expert financial adviser of the commission, often a member of the sinking fund board, and takes an active part in preparing the budget. It is therefore provided, in one case at least, that no warrant for the payment of a claim shall be issued by the city accountant until such warrant is countersigned by the city manager as well as by the head of the department incurring the expense. Furthermore, "each order of purchase or sale," is "to be approved and countersigned by the city manager or his deputy" before the city purchasing agent can close a purchase or contract. The letting of contracts in this same charter is checked by the necessary approval of the city manager and commission before the award can be made, whenever the contract is for an amount over $500. This same charter provides that the city manager shall be a member of the board of revision of assessments; this is certainly an excellent provision for it gives the city manager an intimate knowledge of the income of the city on the side of taxation.

No other charter provides so liberally for control by the expert. It commends itself as a most sensible provision, for it gives the controlling agent in the government the whip hand to get results. Under the old system remonstrance or removal—if removal were ever accomplished when the culprit had political friends—was the sole means of relieving inefficiency. The city's money is paid for results, and if in the judgment of the man seeking them, they are not being obtained, there should be less pay or no pay. It is characteristic of the new order that employees are hired to produce, and not to become merely of more or less decorative value.

Appointive Power.—It will also be noticed that his appointive power is very generous in all the charters. For instance, in Hickory, North Carolina, he furnishes a list of candidates from which are selected officers and employees, in the police, fire, street, waterworks and sewerage departments. This provision is weaker than those usually made and does not seem to be in keeping with the spirit of the plan. The officials so appointed are only to hold office for the meager tenure of one year, and that is probably not long enough for the personnel to take hold heartily of their work as a permanent thing or devote their best energies to it. It also makes difficult the securing of really competent men, for a competent man does not like to have his best efforts cut off at the very time when they are beginning to bear fruit. If the manager is to be responsible, he should be entitled to a chance to do things right as well as a chance to do things wrong which would bring blame upon him. Under this plan he is responsible, without having the power to do things which would make him justly liable, for his employees are in large measure not of his appointing, and those who are, are only there for a short period.

In Dayton, the city manager appoints two general classes of men. The class of major executives serve as heads of departments, as the city attorney, director of public service, director of public welfare, director of public safety, and director of finance. He also appoints the minor executives or those subordinate to the heads of departments, as the health officer, chief of police, fire chief, city accountant, city treasurer and purchasing agent. He may generally select for his employees men resident anywhere. He is expected to achieve efficiency and there is no restriction as to the place in which he may seek a competent man to fill the position he has in mind.

In Springfield, all others than those appointed by the commission and enumerated in a prior discussion of that body, are appointed by the city manager. Springfield has not gone as far in her charter as other charters have in the freedom of appointment which is usually conferred upon the chief executive. For the same reason that there is an error in the charter of Hickory, North Carolina, there is an error in the Springfield charter in restricting the manager in this fashion, for his appointive and removal power is a very potent thing to enable him to secure the results the city expects him to achieve.

In La Grande, Oregon, the city manager appoints

the city recorder, city treasurer, city attorney, chief of police, fire chief, city engineer, superintendent of waterworks, health officer and street superintendent. These men are subject to recall by him, with or without cause.

In Phœnix, Arizona, the city manager appoints the city clerk, city treasurer, city assessor, city collector, city attorney, engineer, chief of police, fire chief and superintendent of streets.

Location of Appointive Power.—In this particular the prudence of the framers of the Dayton charter is exhibited. This scheme of division of powers, set forth in that charter, justly entitles it to the claim of preëminence over all other contemporaneous charters. What more in keeping with the innate justice and businesslike spirit which pervades the new order than to hold the city manager responsible for the complete execution of the trust which is devolved upon him as a public servant? We concentrate the power in him and we look to him to justify our confidence. Yet this very spirit of righteous justification would be a mockery of itself if we did not put it in the power of the man to whom we apply such an acid test to discharge ably the tasks he assumes. The means of discharging the trust must inevitably lie in the personnel of the departments over which he exercises so radical a control. The Dayton charter, therefore, provides that the city manager shall have a very wide and generous scope to his appointments. He has absolute control over his departments, and absolute power of appointment and removal, with or without cause, provided only that he does not act in conflict with the civil service regulations. It is simply a question of the commercial world of how to produce the best results, and an application of the experience of private enterprises that important executives must not be hampered in their means of effecting tangible achievements. It is evident that this must be inevitably the order of affairs if we expect the city manager to write efficiency with a majuscule.

Conclusion.—In this type of officer, the personnel of the new profession is exemplified. It is a far cry from the day of the inefficient amateur to the precisive professional administrator: the annals of civic progress embrace many a weary recital of sloth and indecision, of bad judgment and wilful carelessness. This must be no more. Sincere efforts are now under way to keep a clean record in the future. Above all and beyond all, the idea that ability to direct a city's destiny is a God-given gift common to the politically chosen is meeting its Nemesis; we are living now in a more sophisticated time when the sugar-plums of political quackery no longer satisfy the jaded popular taste. This nation-wide desire for knowledge and publicity and simplicity is garnering its significant fruits of efficiency, economy, and centralized administrative authority. We are indeed on the threshold of the dawning of a new day for a new profession. May its history record a generous fulfillment of its fortuitous beginnings.

CHAPTER VII

THE DEPARTMENTS

In the new as in the old, the central powers of the state are divided into three departments,—legislative, executive and judicial,—which, in the same qualified sense, are separate and distinct from each other.

HANNIS TAYLOR

A grave difficulty has arisen as to the connection of the departments with the commissions. More or less trouble has been experienced in methods of supervising the several divisions of the municipal organization. The conventional species of commission government provided that the positions of the heads of departments were to be filled by the commissioners themselves: the commissioners were to be directors of departments or be responsible, at least, for them.

Des Moines Plan.—Des Moines, Iowa, provided that the commissioners were to be elected to certain positions which were specified prior to the election, and candidates were to compete for defined positions. The electorate had the privilege of selecting, therefore, particular men for a specified job.

In this is found a fundamental error. It is fallacious for this reason, that it puts upon the people the task of selecting a man in a political way for a position which does not involve any political qualifications and in choosing a man in whose make-up the less politics there is, the more efficacious will be his work in behalf of the city he is to serve. The problem is not only the selection of a commissioner, in this form of commission government, but it is also that of selecting an executive; this dual requirement is one fraught with hazard and confusion, and with inevitable difficulty in the exercise of a conscientious and successful selection by the voter of the right man for the right place. These two qualifications of legislator and executive required in a candidate for commissioner will, without doubt, be irreconcilably confused and neither the general results of efficient management nor the personnel of the commission will be what could have been had if the respective positions of the commissioner, as an adviser, and the head of the department, as an executive, were kept separate.

Galveston Plan.—In the Galveston plan, while each commissioner does not actually take part as a director of a department, discharging the details that that position entails, yet he is responsible for that department, and there lies upon him the duty to appoint a competent head who will perform the services required. To each commissioner is allotted the tasks appurtenant to a division of the government, and to each commissioner attaches the difficulties and embarrassments of that department. The commissioner is virtually an executive as well as a legislator. Further, it is to be determined by vote, among the commissioners who are elected to office which ones among them will administer particular departments. This procedure is again liable to wise objections. First, the responsibility for the execution of the duties of the departments is split into as many parts as there are commissioners. There is no one legislative body and no one entire and consolidated executive branch which the people can directly look to and require to produce the requisite results. Second, it is or may be, a matter of injustice to some of the commissioners, for perchance a number of them will fail in their duties while one or two will do well; those who do well will be hampered in their policies on the one hand and hampered in their execution of their duties on the other hand, and it will be difficult to show in what division of the work there was error, whether it was committed through the vote of the majority of the commissioners on the legislative side or the mismanagement of some particular commissioner on the executive side. If these departments, then, are administered separately from the commission the people can see whether mistakes are due to legislation or the fault of execution, and act and recall accordingly.

City Manager Plan.—The city manager plan has a provision of sterling wisdom to meet this situation. It obviates the theoretical and the practical difficulty of combining two radically different phases of any administration work. The commissioners have nothing to do with the execution of the legislation; the city manager has everything to do with the execution of the government business. Therefore, it is justly and very wisely provided that the city manager shall appoint the heads of the departments. The departments are thus directed by means independent of the commission. There is one responsible executive head; and that head, in order to justly hold him accountable has, as stated heretofore, complete power of appointment of those subordinate to him, whether they be of major or minor importance. It is true that the field of selection is sensibly curtailed at times to the domain of a prepared civil service list, but his freedom of choice is unrestricted so far as the material extends.

The Departments.—To return to the discussion

of the model charter of Dayton, with its most advanced features so radically in evidence in the arrangement of the departments, it was provided that a director shall head each department. These departments are five in number, entitled law, welfare, service, safety and finance.

Division Scheme.—The very names of the departments are tellingly significant of the new order of municipal life. We are living in a generous age wherein the social mind is turning itself to general organization rather than to minute subdivisions of the government. It is a division along the line of principles rather than a division along the line of miscellaneous facts. We used to have in a great many cities such divisions as the waterworks department, the street department or the treasurer's office. The very multitude of these disjointed and scarcely related divisions of the government made impossible the efficiency that should have been. We are now vigorously assuming a new duty. Municipal government is divided only along those basic lines that its functions naturally resolve themselves into.

Department of Law

First and foremost, then, of these departments, we have the most fundamental of them, that of law. Over this department is placed an able, trained member of the bar, equipped with professional knowledge and balanced by that instructive experience which comes to the competent advocate. The new department is not merely the place for an officeholder, nor the opportunity for a selfishly ambitious young politician; it holds forth generous opportunities for a keen-minded, logical man of sound business and technical training to apply the ideals of his profession to the very acute needs of his community. The new office directs its occupant to advise the city officials and prevent disputes and complications; it requires him to protect the city in the courts and prosecute its rights in those forums; it obligates him to enforce its ordinances and to create a profound respect for ordinances and rulings promulgated by the officials. The new department is generous in scope; it is a tempting opportunity for the man of constructive mind to make a record of service to his community.

The commission or the city manager, or the director of any department, or a board or an officer not included within a department, may require the city attorney's opinion. The latter officer is empowered to take steps to prevent the abuse of corporate powers, the misapplication of funds, or the performance of contracts in contravention of law or those procured by fraud. He can apply to the courts for an order to compel performance of duties by negligent or wilfully dilatory officials. The city attorney is empowered with liberal authority to protect civic rights.

A Suggestion.—There is one rift in this perfect list of duties. Experience with legal departments of many cities has pointed out one thing, that it takes a different type of legal mind to discharge the duties of city solicitor from that required for the discharge of the duties of city attorney. The solicitor is a lawyer concerned chiefly with the disputes of a civil character; the city attorney is a prosecuting officer concerned largely with the criminal branch or the penal side of the legal department. It is for these reasons that the two offices should not be filled by the same person. Experience has taught otherwise. This can be remedied by the appointment of subordinates peculiarly fitted to the several divisions of the work; but smaller cities in which such division would not be justifiable should enact this provision only after keen consideration.

Department of Public Service

Public service is an apt title for the second department. It is an arduous and thankless and tedious task to arouse civic pride and conscientious ambition. Once done, the results are marvelous.

To impress upon the public that in just the proportion that the dust of the streets and the open garbage cans and sluggish canals and the disposition of city refuse are taken care of, in that proportion is the city health improved, is the death rate decreased, is the infant mortality percentage reduced—this is, indeed, an undertaking of sometimes despairing magnitude.

Scope of Duties.—As to the scope and duty of the new department of public service, primarily it is always "subject to the supervision and control of the city manager in all matters." The director of public service manages the construction and maintenance of streets, bridges and viaducts, and the public highways generally; of the sewerage systems and disposal plants, canals, and water courses; of the public buildings; of the boulevards and squares and city grounds, except those devoted to parks and playgrounds; of the market-houses and farms and public utilities of the city. The head of this department is empowered to enforce all obligations of privately owned or operated public utilities enforcible by the city. And upon him devolves the duty of making and preserving surveys, plans and drawings, and estimates for public work. He also sees that the streets which he maintains and repairs are cleaned, lighted and sprinkled, and that the waste is collected and disposed of. He preserves whatever implements and documents are incidental to the prosecution of work in his department.

Department of Public Welfare

Akin to the department of public service is the department of public welfare. The citizen of twenty-five or fifty years ago in what was then a modern city would undoubtedly be horrified at the social program which the modern municipality undertakes. It is a far cry from that day when Glasgow took the sensible and what was considered a most advanced stand that the hallways and stairways of tenements were in the nature of public thoroughfares and should be lighted and regulated accordingly, to this present day when the scope of municipal control has been so enlarged—in the light of what modern cities are attempting to do under the name of public welfare, the Dayton charter. In fact none of the recent charters under the city manager plan can be accused of being over-radical: they embody many progressive features, but they are well tried. By comparison the city manager charter provisions appear very wise and conservative and sane. For an instance of advanced ideas, Kansas City, Missouri, operates a municipal farm for city prisoners, a women's reformatory where productive work is turned out, a parole department, a recreation department for the inspection of public amusements, a legal aid bureau, a department for the homeless and the unemployed, a social service department for the consolidation and administration of all charities, a research bureau for the scientific investigation of social problems, a factory inspection department and bureau of labor statistics, a welfare loan agency, and a child welfare department.

Powers.—The definition of public welfare is therefore a term of considerable range. The new department under that name in Dayton has the following proposals in view; but whether they will be interpreted to cover any of the above is a matter that time only will clearly answer. All correctional and reformatory institutions and agencies belonging to the city are to be administered by this department; parks, playgrounds and recreational centers of the city are to be controlled by this division. The director has charge of the inspection and supervision of public entertainments; of the enforcement of laws and ordinances relative to the public health in both the prevention, isolation and cure of diseases. Co-related with this is the duty of inspection of the production and transportation, storage and sale of food. In order that the department may be conducted on a system based on scientific knowledge, an accurate analysis of vital statistics is to be kept, and a research into the causes of poverty, delinquency, crime and disease will be conducted. Acting upon the age-old belief that prevention will outweigh in merit even the cure, there will be instituted a program of public education on matters that affect the public welfare, whether it be a matter of crime or health or delinquency. The usual department of health is a subdivision of this larger department of welfare.

Department of Public Safety

Under the director of public safety are the divisions of police and fire. In addition to the general duties of supervision over these two divisions, the director is the chief administrative authority in all matters affecting the regulation of the erection of buildings, their inspection, maintenance and occupancy, as the commission or general code of Ohio may prescribe. Within the scope of this department there is also placed the enforcement of all laws and ordinances relating to the subject of traffic, weights and measures.

The latter provision evidences the principal fault in the Dayton charter, a fault due to the pressure under which the commissioners worked in drafting the instrument. As a logical consequence the charter in places is heterogeneous in character. It would seem that more mature and careful thought would suggest that the subject of weights and measures should be placed under the control of the department of public welfare. This division of municipal government has a kindred subject, as for instance, the control of markets and foodstuffs, and the charter specifically provides that this department shall "supervise . . . sale of foodstuffs." It would therefore be highly commendable to follow the original and basic idea upon which the charter was founded and group similar duties, requiring methods that are akin and appliances that are of the same character, in order that there should be a minimum of conflicting effort in the departments and a minimum of duplication of apparatus. This conglomerate assignment of work among the different departments has been the cause in the past, in other municipal organizations, of much maladministration.

Divisions of Fire and Police

Rules and regulations are made by the chief of police for the control of his department. The city manager determines the number of men in the division. The director of public safety is granted the power to appoint additional men for temporary service, as in the case of riot, who need not be in the classified service. A similar provision is embodied in this governing instrument to take care of the fire department. The suspension of the chief by the manager is reviewed and finally passed upon by the commission after a full and complete hearing. The chiefs of fire and police are subject to removal exclusively by the city manager for the enumerated causes of incompetency, insubordination and immorality.

Department of Finance

The organization of the department of finance under the Dayton charter is the product of genuine constructive thought. A very generous share of credit is due the framers for the excellent system they have devised. Because of its critical character it is set forth here with some elaboration. The system is worthy of emulation.

Simplicity: Uniformity.—The initial step in the organization of such a department is the enactment of an ordinance by the commission requiring a specified type of ledgers, uniform in character; unit cost records; operation reports; and an entire unified system of accounting procedure. Such an ordinance is the criterion of the effectiveness of the new government. The administrators of the city manager plan do not propose to follow the customary idea of running a city on the basis of the cash received and disbursements made, but rather to place the system on the basis of the liability the city will incur. The new government is launched with a determination to stop the waste and have the records of each transaction kept up-to-date and scientifically accurate.

Powers of Director.—The general duties of the director of finance are five in number. First, he is to keep and supervise all accounts; second, he has the custody of all the public money of the city; third, the purchase, storage and distribution of supplies needed by the various departments are under his direction; fourth, the making and collection of special assessments are left to his judgment; and fifth, the issuance of licenses and the collection of fees are also among his duties.

City Accountant.—The supervision of accounts is under the control of an officer styled the city accountant, a member of the force responsible to the director of finance. The accountant supervises the financial transactions and records of all departments and of all the officers of the municipality. Daily departmental reports of money received and disbursements made come into his office; and in standard form all current financial and operating statements are prepared. These statements set forth succinctly the minute details of each transaction and the cost thereof. It is a part of the spirit of the modern municipality to run it like a business and to know where the public corporation stands financially at any moment, rather than follow the ancient method of haphazard expenditure by each department irrespective of the action of any other department, irrespective of the amount of money that was actually in the treasury, or probably would be, and irrespective of economy or any system of accounting. Uniformity of accounting was generally an unknown art in former days in the management of a public corporation.

Accounting Procedure.—A whole system of accounting should be devised to afford the city a history in detail of every piece of business involving the acquisition, custodianship and disposition of values, including the items of cash receipts and disbursements. The same system, as suggested above, for a careful, analytical and scientifically accurate statement, is provided in the section on accounting procedure in the Dayton charter. The basic idea

SPRINGFIELD, OHIO, CITY MANAGER PLAN.

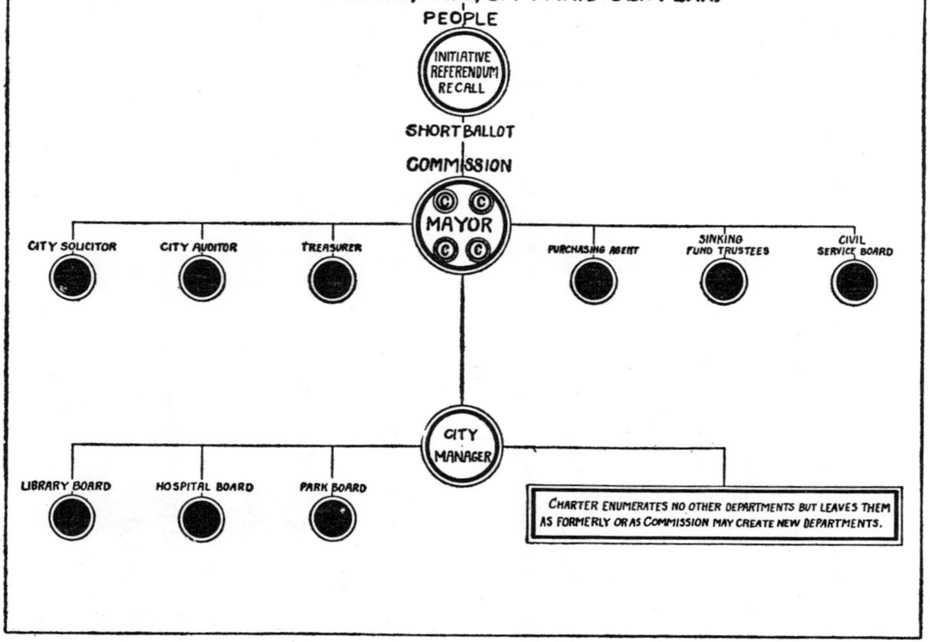

contained in this short paragraph is of peculiar importance to everyone interested in the formation of a charter, for such a system as proposed goes to the very heart of the matter and is the open door to the final successful management of the business of a public corporation with its millions of dollars of assets. It should not seem such a strange and remarkable phenomenon that accounting procedure should have an intimate relation with the success of a city, but the old governments made it conspicuous by its absence. This city accountant has the still further duty of the preparation and certification of all the special assessments for public improvements, the notification of property owners, and the collection of such assessments.

Five fundamental objects should be accomplished in the formulation of a new budget:

1. Appropriations should be based upon detailed estimates.

2. The public hearings upon the estimates should be granted.

3. Appropriations should be kept within the estimated income.

4. The budget should be prepared scientifically, but the proposal should be very plainly stated so that it can be easily understood by the average citizen.

THE DEPARTMENTS

5. Public hearings on the tentative budget in its final form should be required.

The salutary effect of such requirements is self-apparent.

The object of the accounting procedure in Dayton as expressed by the new charter is "to record in detail all transactions affecting the acquisition, custodianship, and disposition of values, including cash receipts and disbursements; and the recorded facts shall be presented periodically to officials and to the public in such summaries and analytical schedules in detailed support thereof."

City Treasurer.—The custody of public funds is left to an official styled the city treasurer. All moneys collected are paid to him and all moneys disbursed must pass through his hands upon proper warrant issued by the accountant under the supervision of the director of finance. The payment of claims by this warrant is only achieved by evidencing the debt through a voucher approved by the head of the department for which the indebtedness is incurred, and countersigned by the manager; and then the city accountant issues the warrant which is to be honored by the city treasurer. This is an admirable system of checks at a point where the doctrine of checks and balances is really needed. Before the head of a department issues a voucher he is presumed to have inspected the material or work in payment of which the voucher is given.

Purchasing Agent.—The best evidence of progress is the newly created office of a general purchasing agent. In private corporate affairs, the purchasing agent is one of the most valuable adjuncts to commercial success that the company may employ. His position is fundamental, for upon his skill and sagacity in trade and his ability to secure bottom prices is based the first calculation of what the ultimate price of the commodity will be.

Yet what private business found its chiefest necessity, public business long maintained it could do without. The modern city no longer finds this so. The exigencies of present commercial methods made indispensable a man who could "purchase all supplies for the city, sell all real and personal property of the city not needed or unsuitable for public use or that may have been condemned as useless by the director of a department. He shall have charge of such storerooms and storehouses of the city as may be provided by ordinance, in which shall be stored all supplies and materials purchased by the city and not delivered directly to the various departments, and he shall inspect all supplies delivered to determine quality and quantity and conformance with specifications, and no voucher shall be honored unless the accompanying invoice shall be indorsed as approved by the city purchasing agent."

In one charter this official requires from the director of each department, at such times as contracts for supplies are to be let, a requisition for the quantity and kind of supplies to be paid for from the appropriation of the department. Upon learning that the funds are available, the agent will purchase in this manner, unless, of course, there presents itself an opportunity to buy goods for cash at a great advantage; thereupon the purchasing agent is at liberty to avail himself of this commercial opportunity and can buy for cash to the credit of the store's account. These supplies so purchased will be furnished ultimately to the department needing them; when the need becomes apparent, such department will requisition what it desires and accompany the requisition with a warrant made payable to the credit of the store's account.

No supplies are to be furnished any department unless there is money in the treasury to that department's account ready to pay for them. There must be to the credit of the department requisitioning them an available appropriation balance in excess of all unpaid obligations, sufficient to pay for such supplies.

Further than this, before purchase or sale, the

city purchasing agent must give opportunity for competition among those able to furnish the supplies, and receive proposals based upon precise specifications under such rules and regulations as the commission establishes. As a further very valuable check, the city manager must approve and countersign each order of purchase or sale. Of course, in case of emergencies, a purchase can be made without competition if there is sufficient appropriation already at hand and a copy of the order issued is filed with the city purchasing agent and attached to the voucher.

In Staunton, the city manager is the purchasing agent, as he is designed to be in Springfield. Actually, however, Mr. Ashburner's private secretary is now discharging the duties of that position. In the latter city, the manager's enumerated duties are generally the same as in Dayton, the plan of which has just been given in substance.

The need of a purchasing agent is demonstrated by the conditions prior and subsequent to the creation of his office. Prior to his advent, it was customary for the head of a department to make out an order, the auditor would sign it, but would not debit the books; the departmental head bought the supplies; yet there was no systematic inspection, there was no system, no anticipation of future conditions or prices, no advantage derived from wholesale prices; all of which might easily have been done if there had been the needed concentration of power and adequate knowledge obtained of the market in which the purchase was made. As a consequence, retail rates were frequently paid, when wholesale could have been secured; there was no comprehensive information as to outstanding bills; appropriations exceeded income, because there was little relation known between what was needed, what was in the treasury, and what could be afforded. Dayton alone faced the average deficit of $60,000 per year. What a stinging indictment of inefficiency!

Look at the present plan! The first requirement is that a requisition must be first made upon a fully informed official, the purchasing agent; then there will be a debiting of the proper account by the auditor; the money must be to the credit of the department making the requisition; the goods are purchased at wholesale whenever possible and always properly inspected; the whole transaction is finally checked by the necessity of the voucher being countersigned by the city manager.

Instances under the old plan of extravagance and waste are startling. The city of Dayton paid $.75 per quart for ink, while the school board paid $.41

at the same time with no reason for difference in price. It has been demonstrated that a saving of 34 to 45 per cent. can be effected by the introduction of the modern methods. In Cincinnati alone a purchasing agent in one year saved the city $100,000. It is expected the sum of $167,000 will pass through the hands of the Dayton purchasing agent, upon which he can exercise his saving abilities. Here is an opportunity for an efficiency record to be made by a competent man.

Certification of Funds.—There is a sound business maxim to the effect that a debt should not be contracted until the money is in sight to pay for it. Dayton proposes to better the maxim. It has provided that the money must be in the treasury before any contract, agreement or other obligation entailing the disbursement of money shall be entered into, or any ordinance or other order to that effect shall be passed by the commission or authorized by an officer of the city, unless the director of finance certifies to the person about to transact the affair that the requisite amount of cash is in the treasury, credited to the fund, appropriated for that purpose, and ready to be expended when the service is rendered. This certificate must be immediately recorded and the sum certified cannot be reappropriated until the obligation is discharged.

Money in Treasury.—This involves the definition of what is money in the treasury to the credit of the fund. The answer is a dual one: first, all moneys are so regarded which are anticipated to come into the treasury before the maturity of the agreement, from taxes or sales or credits in favor of the city; and second, all moneys applicable to the payment of the obligation which have already been paid into the city treasury prior to the maturity of the contract, when derived from the sale of property or bonds.

As to this the Dayton charter says: "All moneys actually in the treasury to the credit of the fund from which they are to be drawn, and moneys . . . anticipated to come into the treasury . . . shall be considered in the treasury to the credit of the appropriate fund."

The arrangement of departments under the city manager plan is notable for one thing in this evolution of city governments. A return has been made to the old doctrine of the division of powers; legislative and executive functions are to be kept apart. Too often reformers believe all that is old is evil; the truth of the matter more frequently is that it is not the idea which is useless, but the application of the idea to modern conditions. The scheme of separation of legislative and executive powers is fundamentally correct; the utilization of the plan in the "old order" was simply proved to be wrong. The present adoption prophesies more pleasing results.

CHAPTER VIII

FINANCE MEASURES

Efficiency in municipal administration means doing the things which the citizens of the municipality want done as well as possible at the smallest possible expense.
WILLIAM A. PRENDERGAST

The heart of a business administration of a municipality is its budget. In just that proportion of excellence which the budget contains, in that proportion the organization will be sound in a commercial sense. The newer forms of government have derived much of their merit from a strict investigation of their finances and a thoughtful, sane provision for their future monetary condition.

The Vital Elements.—The major considerations are sources of income and objects of expenditure. The city must be placed upon a basis where assets and resources are accurately ascertained, where costs are predetermined, where expenditures are made for one thing once, where wholesale prices and uniform purchases can be made in the interest of economy.

Income Classification.—A practical form of classification used in Dayton for estimated income is as follows:

Taxes:
  General
  Liquor Traffic
  Cigarettes

Licenses:
  Vehicle
  Venders
  Theaters and Shows
  Dogs

Permits:
  Water and Sewer
  Other

Excise Taxes:
  Street Railways
  Electric Company

Markets
City Scales
Parks
Public Buildings
Work House
Municipal Court

Interest on Deposits
Public Ways—Miscellaneous
Fire and Police
Inspection Food Products
Refund Arc Lights
Sweeping Tracks
Refunds Cuts in Pavements
Temporary Loans
Water Works Income
Estimated Balances
 Total

Objects of Expenditure Classification.—A similarly useful classification was employed by Mayor Hunt in the 1913 budget of Cincinnati, and was also employed in Dayton to show objects of expenditure. It is:

1. PERSONAL SERVICE
    a. Salaries and wages. (The number of employees and rate of wage under each title or grade shown in detail. Temporary employees shown separately with the rate of wage and number of days of proposed service.)
    b. Fees, commissions, etc., for special service

2. TRANSPORTATION SERVICE
    a. Hire of horses and vehicles, with or without drivers
    b. Transportation of persons
    c. Storage of vehicles
    d. Shoeing and boarding horses
    e. Other transportation service (specified by name)
3. COMMUNICATION SERVICE
    a. Telephone
    b. Postage, telegraph and messenger
4. SPECIAL CONTRACTUAL SERVICE
    a. Repairs by contract or open-market order
    b. Printing (reports, etc.) and advertising
    c. Light and power
    d. Other special contractual services (specified by name)
5. SUPPLIES AND MATERIAL
    a. Stationery and office supplies
    b. Stable and automobile supplies
    c. Fuel
    d. Forage
    e. Provisions
    f. Material
    g. Other classes of supplies (specified by name)

6. Purchase of Land, Structures and Equipment
   a. Furniture and fixtures
   b. Vehicles
   c. Horses and other livestock
   d. Other equipment
   e. Land
   f. Structures (buildings, streets, sewers, bridges, etc.)

7. Fixed Charges and Contributions
   a. Debt service
      1. Interest
      2. Sinking fund installments
   b. Rent
   c. Pensions and contributions
   d. Insurance and taxes
   e. Court costs and reimbursements
   f. Refunds and reimbursements
   g. Other fixed charges and contributions (to be specified)

Advantages of Classification.—The Dayton Bureau of Research quotes Mayor Hunt as advocating this classification for the reasons here presented:

"To make each appropriation item so definite that its purpose may be clearly ascertained.

"To prevent, by proper classification and arrangement, the duplication of requests and appropriations for the same item of expense.

"To provide ready money for determining whether items requested in one department may more properly belong to another department better equipped to handle the special work concerned.

"To afford the best possible opportunity for administrative officers to present definite and convincing evidence of the needs of their several departments; and to make it possible for Council to require such evidence of administrative officers.

"To provide a ready means of comparing specific items of actual expense with specific items of requested appropriations.

"To furnish the Auditor with means for deciding definitely whether or not claims presented to him for audit are properly chargeable to the several appropriation items.

"To state definitely the number of employees and the rate of compensation for which each item of salaries and wages is requested; and thereby enable the Auditor to require the certification and approval of payrolls for payment in such form as to hold officials so certifying responsible for the truth or falsity of the facts certified to.

"To make possible a strict enforcement of the law which limits the incurring of liabilities to the amounts of the several appropriation items.

"To enable Council to ascertain whether or not money is spent for the purposes contemplated in the appropriation.

"To make it possible, by means of a 'functional' classification of items under each organization unit, for Council to pass intelligently upon each question of general policy involved in the consideration of the budget; and for the Mayor to approve or disapprove items in the budget with due regard to efficiency in the public service as it affects the health, education, safety, recreation and convenience of the community.

"To make it possible for Council, the Mayor, and citizens, by utilizing summary statements, *to consider the budget as a constructive community program,* and not merely as unrelated appropriation items; and to determine the relative public importance of each function and activity, in the general administrative scheme of the city government.

"To furnish the basis for the fullest and most intelligent consideration by Council, the Mayor, citizens, taxpayers and the public press, of the financial and social program contemplated in the budget."

Official Reports.—A competent understanding from even a casual survey of the financial condition of a typical city like Dayton prior and subsequent to reorganization is best founded upon the official reports.

1913 Auditor's Report.—The following is a verbatim copy of the nucleus of the auditor's report of the financial condition of the city in the year 1913, that is, prior to the installation of the new government:

ACTUAL FINANCIAL RESULT OF THE CITY FOR THE YEAR 1913

Ordinary receipts, as above, from taxation and
  other sources, not including money borrowed. $1,578,737.01
Ordinary expenditures, as above, for operation
  and maintenance (running expenses)......... 2,037,297.95
Deficiency of ordinary receipts for the year...   458,560.94

SCHEDULE A–III

Exhibit of receipts and expenditures, ordinary and extraordinary, grouped according to functions.

ORDINARY

Grand Divisions of Municipal Functions	Receipts	Expenditures
General government..........	$8,608.02	$122,487.71
Protection of life, health and property.................	7,349.18	358,567.49
Public service...............	254,527.03	463,855.13
Public indebtedness.........	9,455.89	....
Public interest..............	44,327.52	276,028.59
Public taxation.............	1,239,296.06	6,100.04
Special assessments..........	15,153.31	....
Unclassified................	20.00	810,258.99
Total Ordinary..........	$1,578,737.01	$2,037,297.95

EXTRAORDINARY

Extraordinary receipts are derived from sales of city property and from bonds sold.

Grand Divisions of Municipal Functions	Receipts	Expenditures
General government..........	....	$16,299.22
Protection of life, health and property.................	....	14,677.75
Public service	....	494,684.83
Public indebtedness	$1,768,488.63	788,780.00
Special assessments..........	197,990.55	....
Sinking fund investment transactions..................	40,350.00	88,400.00
Total extraordinary......	$2,006,829.18	$1,402,841.80

In view of the financial situation of Dayton, the words "Ordinary" and "Extraordinary" must have been selected by someone with a rare sense of humor. The financial statement set forth above is that of a system which was running the city in debt at the rate of $60,000 per year.

In contrast to this slipshod method of the execution of city affairs, regard the present monetary arrangement. The data here were secured by the new government in coöperation with the Bureau of Municipal Research, the latter body publishing the report of the budget.

Income for 1914.—The estimated income for the year 1914 was calculated at a million and a quarter, as follows:

Taxes:	
General	$604,000.00
Liquor traffic	121,210.00
Cigarettes	600.00
Licenses:	
Vehicle	10,000.00
Venders	3,200.00
Theaters and shows	1,600.00
Dogs	800.00
Permits:	
Water and sewer	7,000.00
Other	1,800.00
Excise Taxes:	
Street railways	2,950.00
Electric company	3,350.00
Markets	25,500.00
City scales	1,300.00
Parks	2,730.00
Public buildings	6,100.00
Workhouse	8,000.00
Municipal court	20,000.00
Interest on deposits	3,870.00
Public ways—miscellaneous	684.00
Fire and police	1,250.00
Inspection food products	1,100.00

FINANCE MEASURES

Refund arc lights............................	$5,000.00
Sweeping tracks.............................	10,000.00
Refunds cuts in pavements..................	10,000.00
	$847,534.00
Temporary Loans............................	125,000.00
Waterworks income	229,000.00
	$1,206,044.00
Estimated balances.....................	43,956.00
Total.............................	$1,250,000.00

Cost Estimates.—The cost by character of expenditures was thus estimated:

	Administration	Operation	Maintenance	Capital Outlay	Total
Supervisory Commission.............	$6,600.00				$6,600.00
Clerk of Commission.	6,625.00			$500.00	7,125.00
Civil Service.........	2,960.00			200.00	3,160.00
City Manager.......	19,600.00			200.00	19,800.00
Department of Law..	12,000.00				12,000.00
Department of Public Service...........	117,482.83	$282,393.80	$125,696.75	37,509.00	563,082.38
Department of Public Welfare..........	19,235.00	110,152.50	18,233.00	6,225.00	153,845.50
Department of Public Safety............	78,356.66	324,557.33	8,708.50	5,925.00	417,547.49
Department of Finance.............	10,325.00	9,200.00		50.00	19,575.00
Municipal Court....	26,166.66				26,166.66
Board of Elections...	18,910.00				18,910.00
Total..........	$318,261.15	$726,303.63	$152,638.25	$50,609.00	$1,247,812.03

or figured as cost by organization units thus:

COST BY ORGANIZATION UNITS

	Salaries	Wages	Total Personal Service	Supplies and Materials	Services Other than Personal	Land, Structures and Equipment	Fixed Charges and Contributions	Total
The Commission............	$6,600.00	....	$6,600.00	....	....	....	....	$6,600.00
Clerk to the Commission...	5,600.00	....	5,600.00	$800.00	$225.00	$500.00	....	7,125.00
Civil Service Board.........	2,400.00	....	2,400.00	400.00	160.00	200.00	....	3,160.00
The City Manager..........	19,100.00	....	19,100.00	400.00	100.00	200.00	....	19,800.00
Department of Law.........	12,000.00	....	12,000.00	....	....	....	....	12,000.00
Department of Public Service:								
Office of the Director.......	6,500.00	....	6,500.00	286.00	197.00	100.00	$57,520.83	64,603.83
Division of Engineering—								
Office of City Engineer.....	5,400.00	....	5,400.00	550.00	100.00	....	....	6,050.00
Bureau of Highways........	....	$8,335.00	8,335.00	....	....	....	....	8,335.00
Bureau of Sewers..........	4,150.00	10,080.25	14,230.25	1,000.00	3,450.00	1,200.00	1,200.00	21,080.25
Division of Streets—								
Office of the Superintendent.	3,400.00	876.00	4,276.00	150.00	100.00	100.00	....	4,626.00
Bureau of Garbage Removal..	....	9,233.50	9,233.50	500.00	16,438.25	1,000.00	....	27,171.75
Bureau of Rubbish and Ash Removal..................	....	23,475.00	23,475.00	300.00	12,520.00	....	....	36,295.00
Bureau of Street Cleaning...	2,200.00	21,172.25	23,372.25	2,770.00	13,950.00	2,357.00	25.00	42,474.25
Bureau of Street Repair.....	....	17,114.00	17,114.00	18,305.00	3,100.00	2,750.00	....	41,269.00
Division of Water—								
Office of the Superintendent.	4,500.00	....	4,500.00	250.00	225.00	100.00	32,628.00	37,703.00
Bureau of Revenue Collection.	10,640.00	3,339.00	13,979.00	1,650.00	325.00	200.00	200.00	16,354.00
Bureau of Pumping and Supply	11,835.00	9,278.20	21,113.20	22,950.00	8,350.00	250.00	....	52,663.20
Bureau of Construction and Maintenance..............	4,825.00	35,798.50	40,623.50	14,200.00	1,700.00	20,600.00	2,000.00	79,123.50
Division of Public Lands and Buildings—								
Office of the Superintendent..	2,000.00	....	....	....	....	....	....	2,000.00

FINANCE MEASURES

Bureau of Lands and Buildings	3,075.00		6,775.00	4,125.00	2,950.00	200.00	235.60	12,285.60
Bureau of Motor Vehicles	3,000.00	800.00	3,876.00	7,050.00	1,050.00	550.00	2,300.00	14,826.00
Division of Street Lighting		876.00			97,722.00			97,722.00
Department of Public Welfare:								
Office of the Director	5,500.00		5,500.00	500.00	1,250.00	1,300.00	3,300.00	11,850.00
Division of Legal Aid	600.00		600.00		25.00	50.00		675.00
Division of Charities							3,000.00	3,000.00
Division of Corrections	7,740.00		7,740.00	9,100.00	500.00	250.00	75.00	17,665.00
Division of Parks and Playgrounds	2,520.00	9,480.00	12,000.00	1,750.00	3,350.00	600.00		17,700.00
Division of Recreation	5,085.00	618.00	5,703.00	1,125.00	3,105.00	860.00		10,793.00
Division of Health—								
Office of the Health Officer	8,020.00		8,020.00	505.00	160.00	710.00		9,395.00
Bureau of Medical Service	7,560.00		7,560.00	2,000.00	600.00	25.00		10,185.00
Bureau of Food Inspection	5,700.00		5,700.00	285.00	165.00	525.00		6,675.00
Bureau of Bacteriology and Chemistry	2,480.00		2,480.00	357.00		50.00		2,905.00
Bureau of Sanitation	3,637.50		3,637.50	525.00		500.00		4,662.50
Bureau of Plumbing Inspection	3,300.00		3,300.00	225.00	120.00	275.00		3,920.00
Division of Hospitals							54,420.00	54,420.00
Department of Public Safety:								
Office of the Director	4,700.00		4,700.00	400.00	50.00	1,700.00	73,206.66	78,356.66
Division of Police	149,530.00		149,530.00	2,700.00	1,400.00		1,100.00	156,430.00
Division of Fire	148,600.00	2,498.50	151,098.50	15,890.00	3,850.00	3,700.00	75.00	174,613.50
Division of Weights and Measures	1,083.33		1,083.33	100.00				1,183.33
Division of Dog Pound		939.00	939.00			525.00		1,464.00
Division of Pensions							4,000.00	4,000.00
Department of Finance:								
Office of the Director	4,000.00		4,000.00	1,100.00	375.00	50.00	50.00	5,575.00
Division of Accounting	2,700.00		2,700.00					2,700.00
Division of Receipts and Disbursements	5,400.00		5,400.00					5,400.00
Division of Purchasing	3,600.00		3,600.00	300.00	1,500.00		500.00	5,900.00
The Municipal Court	23,066.66		23,066.66	2,200.00	200.00	700.00		26,166.66
The Board of Elections	14,560.00		14,560.00	975.00	575.00		2,800.00	18,910.00
Totals	$517,507.49	$153,913.20	$671,420.60	$115,741.00	$179,887.25	$41,627.00	$238,636.09	$1,247,812.03

Budget of 1914.—In this same report of the budget the quoted explanation inserted here is of keen interest to the student of municipal finance, not only because of its subject-matter but also because of the form in which it is put for ready reference for the busy man to get at and understand. This whole report, of which only a part is quoted here, is a model of simplicity and clearness:

"The city budget for 1914 is based upon detailed estimates which were furnished the city manager by the heads of all departments. To facilitate a uniform classification of these proposed expenditures, and to secure the comparative data prescribed by the charter, the manager invited the coöperation of a budget commission appointed by him, and consisting of the director of finance, chairman; the city treasurer, and the director of the bureau of municipal research.

"The estimates of each departmental division have been divided where necessary into four main groups by character of expenditures:

"*Administration.*—The cost of direction and control which is not directly allowable to operation, maintenance or capital outlays.

"*Operation.*—Costs growing out of the current

service performed by a division of the city government.

"*Maintenance.*—The cost of care and upkeep of physical properties and equipment as distinct from the operation of a division. The essential feature of maintenance is *repair* and *replacement;* the cost of labor and materials devoted to the same.

"*Capital Outlays.*—The cost of acquiring property for continuing use, usually equipment, lands and buildings, or labor and material involved in the creation of the same.

"Under each of these heads appears a uniform expense classification by objects or services purchased, with a uniform code number to facilitate accounting operations.

"*Personal Service*
    A1. Salaries.
    A2. Wages.
    A3. Special Service.

"*Supplies and Materials*
    B1. Stationery and Office Supplies.
    B2. Fuel.
    B3. Provisions.
    B4. Clothing.
    B5. Forage and Stable Supplies.
    B6. Motor Vehicle Supplies.
    B7. Mechanical Supplies.

B8. Cleaning and Toilet Supplies.
B9. Medical and Laboratory Supplies.
B10. Manufacturing and Jobbing Supplies.
B11. Materials for Lands.
B12. Materials for Buildings and Structures.
B13. Materials for Equipment.
B14. Other Supplies by Name.

"*Services Other Than Personal*
C1. Transportation of Persons.
C2. Telephone and Telegraph.
C3. Legal Advertising.
C4. Street Lighting.
C5. Light and Power.
C6. Hire of Vehicles and Teams.
C7. Subsistence of Persons.
C8. Public Entertainment.
C9. Other Contractual Services by Name.

"*Fixed Charges and Contributions*
D1. Pensions.
D2. Donations to Private Institutions.
D3. Rent and Taxes.
D4. Insurance.
D5. Loans.
D6. Interest.
D7. Other Fixed Charges by Name.

"*Purchase of Lands, Structures and Equipment*
E1. Land.
E2. Buildings.
E3. Streets.
E4. Sewers.
E5. Water Improvement.
E6. Furniture and Fixtures (including office and departmental furnishings).

E7. Machinery, Tools and Implements (including instruments and apparatus).
E8. Live Stock.
E9. Vehicles and Harness.
E10. Motor Vehicles.
E11. Other Equipment by Name.

"The last column of the ordinance carries the actual appropriation to the several departments, there being an appropriation for each of the five main expense subdivisions if necessary. A transfer from one appropriation to another is done by resolution of the commission. The middle column shows the allotment of the appropriation transfers within this group being made by the city manager. The first column is from the preliminary estimate and is to support the appropriation granted. For example, the appropriation in Code 125 E7, $2,357 for new equipment. This sum is divided into three allotments, one of which carries the detail of the departmental request.

"This type of budget has these advantages:

"Careful departmental estimates in support of requests.

"Knowledge of expenditures for each type of supply or service.

"Adequate control over expenditures without hampering the activities of the departments."

Financial Division of Manager's Report.—The

results of this financial program, so carefully thought out, analyzed and anticipated, are succinctly set forth in the following extract from the report of the city manager for the first six months of his régime:

"DEPARTMENT OF FINANCE

"DIVISION OF ACCOUNTING

"REDUCED FORCE.—With three less men than formerly the department has transacted ordinary business, and has taken over the issuing of licenses from the mayor's office, and the work of the sinking fund trustees.

"NEW ACCOUNTING SYSTEM.—A new accounting system is being installed which will equal the best now operating in any city. When finished the city will have complete control, not only over current funds, but also over all equipment, stores and permanent property. Dayton will then be one of the few cities of the country having a balance sheet showing the exact financial situation of the municipality.

"INVENTORY OF CITY PROPERTY.—An inventory of all city property, stores and equipment has been made and will appear in the next financial statement. As soon as the accounting system is completed this inventory will be corrected each month.

"Overdrafts Impossible.—It is now necessary that the city accountant certify to the presence of properly appropriated funds before an order for supplies or for services can be placed. This absolutely prevents expenditures in excess of cash and the appropriation.

"Bookkeeping Eliminated.—Each department and the newspapers are now given a monthly statement showing the expenditures, reserve for contracts, and available balance in each appropriation. This system makes unnecessary the keeping of books in the departments, and keeps the public informed as to the condition of public funds.

"City Budget Improved.—The city budget for the year was prepared in great detail and in accordance with a uniform classification in order that the public might know to what end it was proposed to spend funds, the number of city employees, rate of salary and wages, etc. Copies may be had at the office of the Finance Department.

"More Revenues from Licenses.—By enforcing the license ordinances against junk dealers, dance halls, bill posters, and others; and by greater vigilance with peddlers, the receipts from this source have been doubled.

"Division of Receipts and Disbursements

"All Money in One Fund.—By placing all current revenues in one fund, instead of into several separate funds as was required when the city was without home rule, it has been found as yet unnecessary to borrow to meet operating expenses, although $125,000 of floating debt has been paid. While a part of this money will have to be reborrowed in the fall, interest amounting to several thousand dollars has been saved.

"Bills Paid by Check.—Bills against the city are being paid by check, which is mailed to the dealer instead of his coming to the office, saving his time, and that of the office.

"Balances Returned to Sinking Fund.—The state of all bond funds has been investigated and where balances remained, or balances existed over reserves for contracts, these were returned to the sinking fund.

"Errors Corrected.—Errors in sinking fund calculations amounting to over $200,000 have been discovered and corrected. The increase in sinking fund charges of $205,000 over that of 1912, and the unequal distribution of the city debt is handicapping municipal progress. It is to be hoped that some plan of redistribution can be worked out.

"Division of Purchasing

"Purchases Regulated.—The creation of a purchasing division permits of all city supplies being bought in quantities and at the lowest price. No supplies are purchased until the requisition is approved by the department and the city manager.

"Prices Reduced.—By making purchases in quantities and letting orders to the lowest and best bidders prices have been reduced from 10% to 90% over those formerly paid. This division will reduce prices approximately $20,000 during the year.

"Supplies Standardized.—Gradually the quality and the purpose of the supplies and materials bought by the city are being definitely determined, and specifications for the same are being prepared. This permits all dealers to bid on an equal basis.

"Bills Discounted.—Practically all orders issued by the purchasing division provide for a discount of 2% for payment within ten days after the first of the month following.

"Samples of Saving.—Conceding that prices fluctuate from time to time some of the larger savings over former prices are: Printed matter, $1,000; soap, $312; electric lamps, $144; coffee, $102; cylinder oil, $531; coal, $400; meat, $560;

corporation cocks, $700: brass cocks, $200; cast iron pipes, $1,725; fire hose, $1,600."

Reduction of Debt.—In reference to the matter of the reduction of the debt and running expenses, Mr. Waite, of Dayton, has been quoted as saying in September of the first year of his incumbency:

"I believe we have enough to see us through without causing the city any extra indebtedness. Of course we must borrow back part of the $125,000 paid off at the beginning of the year, but as I figure it now I think it is safe to say that we can reduce this debt about $30,000 this year, by saving the interest of about $6,000 and borrowing only $100,000."

And in this connection the departments were cut in running expenses in this manner:

"Welfare, $8,182.66; civil service, $530; clerk of commission, $795; service, $11,260.96; water, $2,977.50; lands and buildings, $1,880; lighting, $200; finance, $1,730; safety director, $3,718.06; police, $3,940; fire, $6,975; hospitals, $3,809.40."

Saving Interest Charges.—A total cut of $5,000 was made. It is to be observed that keen judgment was used when the floating indebtedness was reduced $125,000 at the beginning of the year and some of it reborrowed at the end of the year so that a considerable interest charge could be saved during the interim, instead of carrying the whole debt the whole year.

Conclusion.—It may seem rather absurd to the layman who knows the necessities of a private business and the care with which the financial program must be treated, that a public corporation should so long have neglected this fundamental provision. Budgets have been prepared, it is true, but the general situation of incompetent financial administration remains unchanged. This new plan is not the origin of a scientifically prepared budget, it is true, but it is a plan which requires and makes provision for such a budget and arranges matters so that the public is allowed public hearings upon it and that publicity attends it and that last-minute changes of political manipulators are not possible. These are some of the features of the new government and they afford vital reasons for its success. While we must constantly have in mind that a public corporation is different from a private corporation in the particular of its governmental character, that a public corporation has a dual nature of governmental and proprietary functions, yet in the phase of its private or proprietary character it is no whit alien to the everyday business of any industrial enterprise; the matter of government does not enter into the question.

CHAPTER IX

EDUCATION OF OFFICIALS

A system of general instruction which shall reach every description of our citizens, from the highest to the poorest, as it was the earliest, so will it be the latest, of all the public concerns in which I shall permit myself to take an interest.

THOMAS JEFFERSON

The Problem.—The greatness of a modern state is generated by the vigor of the educational system it has founded. No conception of a social organization which negatives or neglects the fundamental requisite of the adequate education of its members can have hope of any permanent fortuitous achievements. No form of government can achieve substantial solidarity without the beneficent leavening of a systematic training of its citizenship. Education of the people was, in the lofty-visioned mind of its pioneer advocate in a genuine democracy, Mr. Jefferson, the cornerstone of perpetual accomplishment. Not for naught did that canny statesman and keen calculator of human affairs decree that upon his tombstone should ever rest the memorial of his fathering a great endeavor of popular learning to become the capstone of his native state's educational system, as when he elected to be known as the creator of the University of Virginia.

Time has but emphasized the wisdom of his observation. If we desire to proceed to the creation of a new profession of public officials, we must provide the source in arranging for their education. You may be born a citizen, but you must be trained to be a competent official. Experience with the unhappy ignorance, incompetence and inefficiency of past incumbents of official positions teaches us the bitter lessons of unpreparedness of those whom we have elevated to power.

It is stern business, this business of education of men for officialdom. As the new government for cities is presented here, so also is the method for the furnishing of men with training and ability to carry the new burdens. While it will take time to train the new men and much must be accomplished with those individuals who have acquired their training in devious ways without a systematic course, yet, having created the opportunity, we should equally endeavor to see that young men are given the training to adequately fulfill the opportunity for service to themselves and the state without leaving it to the present methods of chance education. Fortunately, the demand is small now, so that those who have been trained at haphazard may suffice for a while, but they are few in number. The future will demand more, and they must be methodically provided.

The Need.—The demands for the new personnel of the new profession will increase not only for commission managers, but others in the ranks of administrators and executives in municipal affairs. Many will answer the call of the tempting opportunities for public service and personal achievement offered. They must be educated to the task. We must provide for the permanent excellence of our new institution. General managers, city or commission managers, may not always be with us in name, but the idea of the plans they represent of enlightened official administration has come to stay. The demand for trained men is an assured thing.

Methods of Education.—This education of those destined to be municipal executives by profession may proceed in two ways. The first is the present method of taking technically trained men with business experience who have been selected or elected to minor municipal positions, have acquired experience and have then been elevated to major administrative duties. We can retain that method, of course. Second, we can arrange the systematic way of providing education in our institutions of learning, as colleges, universities, technical institutes and similar places.

Efforts of Educational Institutions.—Excellent work has been done already by these institutions. They have shown a wise, facile reflection of the popular movement for and a profound interest in enlightened local government. The gospel of a new political life is finding teachers and disciples. Harvard University has founded a Bureau of Research for the training of men to enter this field of municipal investigation. A special series of courses is offered in the Graduate School of the same university for those who desire to become secretaries of commercial organizations and chambers of commerce in the cities. Business law, accounting, industrial organization, business statistics, railroad organization, investments, corporation finance, railway and shipper relationships, European and South American trade, are among the topics studied; a comprehensive program. The particular methods of the commercial organizations themselves are studied, as the securing of industries, trade expansion, adjustment of traffic problems, civic betterment movements, and the what-not of such organizations' multitudinous activities. Actual field work, it is understood, will be undertaken. The whole series of courses will constitute an opportunity for excellent training and experience in a political laboratory.

Active with commendable forethought and wisdom is the University of Texas, at the other edge of the country. A bureau of research, particularly designed to have the dual capacity of training students and furnishing information to city officials, has been created. The Harvard bureau contemplates mainly the training of men. The Texas bureau is under the direction of Professor Herman G. James, of the university School of Government, of which the bureau is a part. Professor James' suggestions and labor for specific training of municipal executives have been of constructive pioneer character and the growth of the new phase of work should have a happy history.

Progress in Late Years.—The interest in municipal government and the provision for its study have been advancing. As the result of an investigation in 1908 by the National Municipal League, it developed that one or more courses, which were wholly devoted to municipal government, were offered in forty-six institutions, and one hundred more institutions touched upon the topic of municipal government in their general courses in political science. Another investigation, upon a larger scale, was launched by the League in 1912. Independent treatment of municipal government had increased in American institutions to the total of sixty-four, the number of courses varying from one to three, and the number of students enrolled varying from five to eighty-six. Fifty-five institutions offered practical work. In this connection, the Intercollegiate Civic League has been doing excellent work in encouraging bodies of students to undertake practical investigations of extensive scope; the accomplishments of the clubs composing this organization have been of a high order under the circumstances.

The Problem of a Systematic Course.—There yet remains any universal effort to establish regular courses or a series of courses leading to specific ends or degrees with the avowed single purpose of the training of the men for official positions. The departments in the universities and colleges of Engineering, Law, Medicine, Architecture, Business Administration, Finance, and graduate work offer many courses available for a suitable combination in conjunction with certain special courses to be added which would turn out able, accomplished executives.

Probable Courses.—In the school of engineering, the topics of municipal engineering, sanitary engineering, civil engineering, engineering architecture, hydraulic engineering, rivers and harbors, housing problems and electrical engineering might be suggested as especially interesting and helpful. Likewise in Law may be included the subjects of municipal corporations, codification, constitutional law, administrative law, police regulations at home and abroad, criminal law, insurance, negotiable instruments, interest and usury; in Medicine, hygiene, public health, sanitation, hospital construction and administration, civic pathology and pathological laboratories, quarantine, preventive medicine, food and dairy inspection, vital statistics; in Finance, accounting, municipal accounting, budget making, taxation, sales and purchase methods, world markets, domestic and foreign trade, banking, bond issues; in Architecture, city planning, housing problems, building codes, landscape gardening, parks; in Business Administration, transportation, traffic problems, efficiency methods, production methods, commercial law. In general academic work emphasis could be laid upon American and European history, economics, studies of foreign trade conditions, political science, publicity organizations, education, mathematics, sciences, foreign languages, social service and philanthropy and studies in crime and poverty. These are but a part of the multitude of subjects, a large division of which is already efficiently taught, and which but remain to be organized into a course extending over a predetermined period leading to some such degree as is now common, for instance, an A. B., A. M., M. D., LL. M., or to a new degree as Master of Public Works, or Bachelor of Municipal Administration.

These courses would ally practical work with the lectures and library investigations. Field work either in winter or summer vacations would be required as practical work is required of students in engineering or agricultural colleges, who go out in summer to the factories or farms and learn to meet actual problems. So it would be with the student of municipal administration. Work in city research bureaus, on investigations and reports during the summer, in commercial organizations, would supplement the regular courses and constitute a part of the requirements to be fulfilled for graduation.

Municipal executives will not, of course, be chosen direct from the ranks of the newly graduated. They must serve as minor officials or in other positions where business and executive experience can be had. How well they acquire and profit by that experience in conjunction with their scholastic activities should determine the rate of their advancement from post to post in the municipal field.

Happily this is no longer the dream of the cloistered fanatic. We have the opportunity for the men, the men themselves, many of the courses already organized, and these but await the final consummation of the complete arrangement of a collegiate course in municipal management. It is to be hoped that the educational institutions will continue their progressive policies and grasp this golden opportunity for public service.

CHAPTER X

ATTITUDE OF LABOR AND SOCIALISM TOWARD THE COMMISSION MANAGER PLAN

> Parliament is a deliberative assembly of one nation, with one interest, that of the whole; where not local purposes, not local prejudices ought to guide, but the general good, resulting from the general reason of the whole.
> — EDMUND BURKE

Introduction.—The labor vote has become a significant factor in municipal politics. Particularly significant does it become when it is organized labor which enlists its compact body in the contest; labor then becomes a unit with precise political pretensions of its own, ascertainable numbers and definite demands which must be accounted for.

As such a vital force, its position toward a change in the method of self-government is one of no mean import. A local machine always counts upon it as one of the recognized legions; the advocate of a change in government can do no less, and must often do a great deal more than the machine if he hopes for a reasonable degree of success in carrying his contention before the bar of the people. That is one reason for accounting for the attitude of labor toward this new plan.

Yet, this is rather the evidence than the cause of why we should regard it closely, with attention and respect. The cause lies in this, that the laboring class, particularly in industrial communities, is composed of large numbers, is more directly concerned by intimate contact and restriction of personal resources with the problems of sanitation, health, hospital, delinquency, housing and crime. The sources of their livelihood, the mode of life of the worker and his opportunities, as well as the usual crowded living conditions make him realize in a more personal way than the other classes of citizens, perhaps, some of the more vital problems of our urban life. For these reasons, among many, their point of view is of keen interest, political, economic, and social, when that point of view is expressive of an attitude toward a radical change in the form of government of one of our basic political units, the city.

Labor has taken a profound interest in the political changes dealing with municipal reform occurring within the last few years. In Des Moines a labor leader became a commissioner, down in Wichita a switchman on a railway was elected to a similar position, as was a barber in Topeka. And the interest of labor has not been sporadic as the steady number of labor candidates and labor men elected attest. That is normal, hopeful and fair. It is encouraging that a class needing representation is interested and properly represented; it is an insurance of the democracy of our new institutions.

So it has been under the city manager plan. Dayton proved the inherent democracy of its new government by electing to the body of commissioners a laboring man, a typesetter. His election was pleasing and significant for this reason, among others, in that it indicated the interest of his constituents, laboring men; in that all classes would have a voice; and in that the laboring man could not complain that his views, his problems, his needs and desires were not presented by a man who understood him, was one of him, was his brother at his daily task; and the laboring man on the board, no matter what his talents and experience in administration, can assist his fellow-commissioners by the contribution of his special knowledge of many phases of city life and the problems of several of the urban classes.

In the choice of a laboring man for the position of commissioner much objection was logically raised in the past, because such a commissioner was, perforce, obligated to perform certain administrative duties which his previous experience, opportunities and training scarcely fitted him for in many instances. This stumbling-block is removed in the city manager plan. The mastery of departmental details, the competent disposal of administrative problems by his personal settlement, the technical knowledge, the business experience, are no longer necessary on the part of the commissioner to the consequent benefit of the city and himself. His election is now more feasible, for the chief objection of his opponent detractors is removed, to the benefit of his constituents. The generality of the charge of administrative inexperience upon the part of the labor candidate is not assumed to reflect upon his ability, but is assumed to meet the opponents of his election upon their own ground, adopting their most pessimistic view of the situation. Under the city manager plan he sits in a position where his sound common-sense and practical judgment may contribute their meed of advantage without diminishing their effect by unwitting blunders; if right, his opinions will sway other fair-minded members of the board while they are deciding upon and formulating policies for the administration of the city's affairs; if wrong, he can be corrected or outvoted. His viewpoint will always be valuable to men conscientiously willing to administer the municipal corporation for the major interests of all the constituent classes comprising its population.

It is in this manner that the city manager plan enlarges the scope of popular choice, silences the assailants of commission government who argue that the feature of a commission is but a measure of "special privilege" rule, and approaches the nearest to a really satisfactory representative government.

With the elimination of the one-man rule of mayor under former governments, the laboring men no longer need fear the dominance of a powerful element who control that mayor and are hostile to the laboring man's interests, leaving him without an effective voice raised in his own behalf. Nor will there be need, in order to secure whatever advantages he desires for himself, and which he ought fairly to have, to trade in councilmen or take part in log-rolling or consistently engage in the dicker of the wards. It should be plainly understood that this plan does not propose to eliminate the necessity of any interest, on the part of labor, as in actually participating in governmental affairs. Nor does it eradicate the vital element of the laboring man's interest, but it does more largely assure that if he is interested, he may nominate, and have a fair chance to elect, and electing his man, know that his choice will be an effective element in the competent administration under which he desires to live. There is always an opportunity for fair play.

In the campaign in Springfield, Ohio, which led to the election of the charter framers, the adoption of the charter, and the election of the commissioner, the Trades and Labor Assembly was officially and actually in favor of the movement, and coöperated with the civic and commercial organizations for the city in the final securing of the results. The presidents of the Trades and Labor Assembly, the Merchants' Association and the Commercial Club formed the working nucleus of the whole reform organization; the new charter with its radical proposals and effective plans for business administration was the one ground of compromise and the adjustment of many difficulties. It was a matter of some profound surprise to several elements of the citizen body who had theretofore regarded themselves as at variance in many particulars, to find that they could meet at the point of both desiring a great many radically good things. The labor interests have continued to take an active part in the new government since the election of the commissioners, and in many particulars, as in the franchise granted to the gas and electric light companies, or the proposed franchises, they have carried on energetic propaganda and representations of their position. Such activity and interest, while it may not always conform to the views of the majority in any community, is a sign of high hope for the success of our new institutions.

The result of the election of the commissioners in Springfield showed that a laboring man, a foreman in a printing shop, and one understood to be an enthusiastic union advocate, was a member of that body. The other members of the board were leading officers of vast industrial enterprises and each one of them was a director in one of the several national banks. The new board therefore assumed a cosmopolitan aspect and insured the representation of alien interests.

In the city of Dayton, labor assumed a somewhat dual position. It was reported at the time, and there was every official evidence of it, that organized labor was bitterly opposed to the city manager plan. The early part of the campaign, and indeed a good deal of the latter part, brought forth a number of instances of this opposition. For instance, the press reported the following resolution as having been passed to indicate the official expression of the laboring man in Dayton. No comment is made upon the contents of this resolution; its interesting character as a document of progressive nature is sufficiently apparent from the arguments appearing upon its face. It is left to stand upon its own merit. It is left to stand upon whatever merit it may contain.

"WHEREAS, the City of Dayton will hold on May 20, 1913, a special election to choose fifteen charter commissioners to draft a new charter for the city; and

"WHEREAS, The Chamber of Commerce, the Manufacturers' Association, and in fact all the organized money interests of the city are actively advocating the so-called City-Manager form of municipal government; and

"WHEREAS, in advocating this plan they have used campaign methods which we condemn, namely, by trying to create the impression that organized labor or a considerable portion of it has indorsed their plan because a 'prominent' member of organized labor has been selected as one of their candidates; and

"WHEREAS, the method of selecting these candidates was automatic and the reverse of democratic, and the candidates were selected absolutely by the

ATTITUDE OF LABOR AND SOCIALISM 163

Chamber of Commerce without consulting the wishes of organized labor or the working class in general; and

"Whereas, we recognize in this City-Manager Plan a conspiracy to overthrow the liberties of the people and place the city government in the hands of the Chamber of Commerce and the big business interests, as has been proved by the history of Commission Government in other cities; and

"Whereas, we recognize in the 'non-partisan' feature of the plan an attempt to increase the cost of running for public office and to make it practically impossible for a workingman to obtain public office except with the support of the employing class; and

"Whereas, the income of the city in the past has been inadequate, owing to the giving away of valuable public franchises to private corporations and the rebuilding of the city will require a greatly increased revenue, and the City-Manager program includes no plan for raising this revenue outside of bond issues as in the past; and in fact their whole appeal is based upon the personal popularity and glory of individuals who became prominent during our recent disaster with which they seek to dazzle and blind the workers to the fact that while they share in none of the glory, the workers themselves must in the end rebuild the city and bear the financial burden as well; therefore,

"Be It Resolved, That we, the United Trades and Labor Council of Dayton, most emphatically condemn the City-Manager Plan as being hostile to the interests of the organized workers and the working class in general, for the following reasons:

"1. The City-Manager Plan comprehends the concentration of both administrative and legislative power in the hands of three men—to this we object.

"2. The underlying principle of the City-Manager Plan, is distrust of the people.

"3. We firmly believe that the mayor should be the chief executive officer of a municipality, and that he should be elected directly by the people.

"4. The City-Manager Plan almost wholly eliminates the possibility of minority representation, which in our judgment is a fatal mistake.

"5. The City-Manager Plan provides that the Commission shall appoint the Civil Service Commission—this is not only objectionable but unjust, giving the appointing power absolute control of the civil service board.

"6. It is built upon an idea imported from a country village, its leading advocates are imported hirelings of unknown interest, it is possible under this plan to import a full corps of city officials from some other city, under the guise of trained administrators.

"7. It can and will lead to the grossest kind of extravagance; no one knows what it will cost our taxpayers and working people.

"8. It is certain to bring into operation a brand of politics more vicious than what we have ever had, which will result in a manager being selected who could not possibly be elected by a majority of votes of the people.

"9. We do not believe in the importing of Professional Promoters to select a plan or men to run our city.

"Be It Further Resolved, That all delegates from organizations affiliated with the United Trades and Labor Council report this action back to their respective organizations, and that a copy of these resolutions be sent to all newspapers of this city with the request that they publish them in full.

"The United Trades and Labor Council indorses all candidates who carry a union card on condition that if elected they agree to support the principles embodied in the United Trades and Labor Council constitution in drafting a new charter for the city of Dayton.

"The following candidates have agreed to do so:
"Dan P. Farrell, carpenter

"W. H. Buzzard, painter
"A. I. Mendenhall, printer
"Gustave Robert, molder
"Chas. B. Grant, plumber
"Chas. J. Fulwiler, pattern-maker
"Willard Barringer, printer
"United Trades & Labor Council
            "FRANK H. SWENY, Sec'y."

It was claimed from some labor sources that this resolution had not been submitted for official sanction and did not express the actual opinions, wills and desires of the laboring class. Observers and actual workers in the campaign who were in daily touch with every movement do not agree that this resolution is representative of labor, and the result at the polls indicates that the attitude of labor was the very reverse of what this resolution would indicate. It is certainly fair to say, from a dispassionate review of the facts, that labor took an active and intelligent part in the campaign. As matters of this sort rest so largely in opinion, it would be out of place to make any comment upon their attitude one way or the other, and one must be content with a record of the facts.

Labor elected one of its number to the board of commissioners. The rank and file, therefore, must have been in greater accord than this resolution predicts. A strong argument during the campaign was made to those laboring men, of whom there seem to be a large number, who owned their homes, or who were in the process of acquiring entire ownership of them, and who had a very substantial interest in progressive administration of city affairs. The opinion of the man who was thus advancing his own interests so commendably by acquiring a home, was of course of more import than that of the man who was a member of the floating class of labor.

No clearer review or estimate of the actual attitude of this force can be had until you also consider the Socialist element. In Springfield, the Socialist party did not play a particularly effective part as an individual factor in the campaigns. In Dayton, they played a noticeable part, but in the final result one that could not be designated as effective. They had much to do with the attitude of the labor element, as the membership in the respective organizations of both labor and Socialism seem to largely overlap. The meetings preliminary to the elections, a vast number of which were held in all sections of the city, were characterized in many instances, as reported, by a great deal of questioning, interested comment, and some heckling on the part of those who presumably held socialistic views. That was normal campaign interest and enthusiasm. They also held meetings of their own or proposed such meetings. Their candidate or leader was reported to have answered that he would have nothing to do with the charter committee because the chairman of that committee had stated that party politics was to be eliminated, the good of the municipality was alone to be considered and that those dealing with the committee would be expected to do so upon those terms. The course adopted by the Socialists was one that necessitated a strict adherence to party lines and party organization. They would have nothing else apparently. The whole spirit of the movement was the elimination of party lines and party politics. The conflict resultant is obvious. Other organizations, in the main, obliterated such distinctions and came into the fold of the general movement for the common good. The chiefest objection the Socialist element advanced to the new charter was the high rate of percentage necessary to start the recall, initiative or referendum. They claimed that the proposals had been thus rendered ineffective. The scheme of preferential voting was vigorously urged. The net result of this opposition by the socialistic organization was that the lowest man proposed by the citizens' committee as a member of the charter commission secured double the vote of the Socialist leader.

In Cleveland, Ohio, in a campaign for a charter where a similar provision as to the initiative and referendum was advanced, the Socialist party favored the scheme. In Sandusky, Ohio, which recently, in August, 1914, adopted a city manager charter, the Socialists were in favor of the plan as a whole, and these articles in particular. The conflict of opinion as thus exhibited in actual practice indicates the enormous difficulty of drawing any conclusive opinion as to the attitude of this force in municipal reform.

CHAPTER XI

CITY MANAGER STATUTES

All power may be abused if placed in unworthy hands.
CHIEF JUSTICE TANEY

From the time when Staunton, Virginia, encountered the obstacle of the state constitution and state statutes, and from the time when the New York legislature rejected the "Lockport plan," the enactment of suitable statutes has been the initial struggle in each state for the right of a city to have a manager. In Ohio, it was not until a new convention was proposed by the constitutional convention in 1912 and enacted by the people, that the city manager plan became a tangible possibility. The chiefest vantage ground of the reactionary forces was in the antiquated provisions of the fundamental laws of each state.

The analyses of the state laws of the following commonwealths have been made by The National Short Ballot Organization and are herewith reproduced through the courtesy of that organization.

"A. THE LOCKPORT PLAN.

[The so-called "Lockport plan" was embodied in a bill introduced in the New York legislature in 1911, but never passed. In form it is a general enabling act applicable to any city of the third class (that is, one having a population of less than 50,000) upon adoption by local referendum, and would have supplemented the special city charter. Many of the sections of the measure have to do with conditions local to New York state and, hence, are only included here by number and title. As the sections dealing with elections and general corporate powers of the city do not belong distinctively to the city manager plan, they are also omitted. This bill has been used as a model for practically all the subsequent city manager charters.]

"*The people of the State of New York, represented in Senate and Assembly, do enact as follows:*

"ARTICLE I.

"GENERAL PROVISIONS.

"Sec. 1. Short Title. This act shall be known as 'The Optional Third Class Cities Law.'

"Sec. 2. The Term City. The term city as used

in this act shall apply only to such cities of the third class as shall adopt or shall seek to adopt this act.

"Sec. 3. Corporate Powers. The corporate powers of the city as defined in the charter are hereby confirmed.

"Sec. 4. Application of This Act. The provisions of this act shall apply to all cities of the third class which shall adopt the same, as a whole, and shall file such notices of the adoption of the same as are herein provided, with the County Clerk of the county in which the city is situated.

"ARTICLE II.

"ADOPTION OF THIS ACT.

"Secs. 5 to 9, Inclusive. [Provisions for submission of the question of adoption by the city to popular vote, record of result of vote, etc.]

"ARTICLE III.

"REORGANIZATION UNDER THIS ACT.

"Sec. 10. First Election under this Act.
"Sec. 11. Term of First City Council.
"Sec. 12. The Period of Reorganization.

"Sec. 13. Redistribution of Corporate Functions.
"Sec. 14. Restrictions on Such Redistributions.
"Sec. 15. Succession of Functions.
"Sec. 16. No New Corporate Power.
"Sec. 17. Organization within Departments.
"Sec. 18. Special Authority to Borrow.

"ARTICLE IV.

"ELECTION AND RECALL OF OFFICERS.

[The text of Secs. 19 to 23, inclusive, follow closely the charter of Berkeley, California (q. v.)]

"Sec. 24. Nomination by Deposit. (1) In lieu of a petition of nomination a deposit of fifty dollars in legal tender may be made by any candidate for the office of alderman and his name shall be entered upon the official ballot in all respects as if a petition had been filed and accepted. The city clerk shall give to such candidate a receipt for such deposit, which shall, in every case, be sufficient evidence of the payment therein mentioned.

"(2) The sum so deposited by any candidate shall be returned to him in the event of his obtaining a number of votes at least equal to fifteen per centum of the number of votes cast for any candidate elected. Otherwise such sum shall belong to the city for its public uses.

"(3) The sum so deposited shall, in the case of the death of any candidate after being nominated and before the election, be returned to the legal representative of such candidate.

"ARTICLE V.

"THE CITY COUNCIL.

"Sec. 25. Legislative Power Vested. The legislative and general regulative powers of the city shall be vested in a city council which shall consist of five aldermen elected at large. There shall be no other elective officers of the city.

"Sec. 26. Term of Aldermen. The term of aldermen shall be four years, subject to recall by the voters of the city, as hereinbefore provided by this act.

"Sec. 27. Resignations. Any alderman may resign at any time and his office shall be filled by the remaining members.

"Sec. 28. Qualifications. The qualifications of aldermen shall be the highest non-professional or non-technical qualifications specified for any officer under the charter.

CITY MANAGER STATUTES

"Sec. 29. Compensation. Aldermen shall receive such salary, if any, as is granted by the charter. But the city council may determine upon an amount which they may consider a just and adequate compensation for their public services and may submit a proposition to the qualified electors of the city, at any regular or special election, to fix their compensation in that amount. Such proposition shall be submitted in the following form: 'Shall the compensation of aldermen be fixed at (insert amount)?' If a majority of the electors voting shall vote affirmatively on such proposition, the salaries shall be fixed accordingly, to take effect on the first day of the calendar month next succeeding the official canvass of the vote and shall not be refixed except by the same process.

"Sec. 30. Eligibility for Other Offices. No alderman shall be eligible for any other municipal office during the term for which he shall have been elected, except in such ex-officio capacities as are provided for in this act, for which he shall receive no additional compensation. The acceptance of any other public office shall operate to vacate his membership in the city council.

"Sec. 31. Meetings of City Council. (1) The city council shall meet for special purposes at all such times as are fixed therefor by the charter.

"(2) An ordinance shall be passed, before this act shall be declared to be in full operation, providing a schedule of regular sessions to occur not less frequently than is fixed by the charter, and for the special sessions at which the city council shall act in the capacity of Board of Estimate and Apportionment and as the ex-officio governing board of any corporate bodies within the municipality as hereinafter provided.

"(3) Any two members may call a meeting.

"(4) All meetings shall be public.

"(5) Any citizen may have access to the minutes upon application to the city clerk.

"CITIZEN'S MOTION.

"(6) Any citizen may appear before the city council at any of its regular meetings and may present a printed motion. Said motion shall be acted upon by the city council, in the regular course of business, within fifteen days.

"Sec. 32. Quorum. Three members shall constitute a quorum to transact business, but a smaller number may adjourn from day to day and compel the attendance of absent members.

"Sec. 33. Passage of Measures. Three votes shall be required to pass any measure involving the expenditure of money, confirming appointments or removals, granting a franchise, or authorizing a bond issue. A simple majority shall suffice for the passage of any other measure. The signature of the mayor shall not be required in any case.

"Sec. 34. No Member Excused. No member shall be excused from voting except on matters involving the consideration of his own official conduct. In all other cases a failure to vote shall be entered on the minutes as a negative vote.

"Sec. 35. Mayor to Preside. The mayor shall preside at all sessions and shall have two votes in case of a tie.

"Sec. 36. Succession of Functions. The city council shall succeed, severally and collectively, to all such powers, duties and penalties for non-performance or malfeasance, as are conferred, imposed or inflicted upon common councils and aldermen and councilmen in cities of the third class by the general laws of the state and the charter, and are not inconsistent with the provisions of this act. They shall likewise succeed to all the powers heretofore exercised by the several officers and boards of the city government, except as hereinafter specified. And it is further provided that the limitations laid down in the charter and in the general laws of the state with regard to the exercise of powers and duties by the several administrative officers and boards, shall be applicable to the exercise of the said powers and duties by the city council, when said city council shall succeed to the said powers and duties, in so far as said limitations are not in conflict with the provisions of this act.

"Sec. 37. Powers and Duties of City Council enumerated.

"Sec. 38. Control Over Administrative Departments.

"(1) The city council shall have power and it shall be their duty to issue general and special orders, by resolution, to the city manager, giving him authority to carry out, in accordance with law, the administrative powers and duties conferred and imposed upon the city.

"(2) They shall require the city manager to present, once a year, a complete report, financial and otherwise, of the activities of the several departments of the city government, and special reports at any time.

"(3) In cities where the charter provides for a Board of Estimate and Apportionment, that body shall consist of the city council meeting in special session, public notice whereof shall have been given as provided by Sec. 31 of this article. At such special session the city council may compel the attendance of all heads of administrative departments, and shall exercise the functions designated to the Board of Estimate and Apportionment by the charter.

"(4) The city council may provide for a board of audit, or a special auditor, to be directly subject to their control, and independent of the city manager. Such board or officer shall have access to all vouchers and other public records within the several administrative departments at all times and shall have such powers consistent with the law as the city council may confer. But all claims arising from injury to person or property shall be audited and disposed of by the city council.

"(5) The city council shall have power to validate any lawful act performed by any administrative officer of the city without its previous authority.

"(6) In cities which are independent highway districts the city council shall be ex-officio commissioners of highways.

"Sec. 39. Agents of the State Government. Whenever the city council shall, in pursuance of the provisions of this act, assume the functions of boards which are essentially the local agents of the state administration, they shall be amenable to the central administrative officer or body to the full extent of the powers granted and the duties imposed by the operation of this act.

"Sec. 40. Effect of Enumeration. The enumeration of any power or powers herein granted the city council shall not be construed so as to exclude any others which may be granted by any other law applicable to the city and not inconsistent with this act. The exercise of powers by the city council shall be subject to the provisions of Article XI.

"ARTICLE VI.

"THE MAYOR.

"Sec. 41. How Chosen. The mayor shall be that member of the city council, who, at the regular election of officers, shall have received the highest number of votes. In case two candidates receive the same number of votes, one of them shall be chosen mayor by the remaining three members elected to the city council. In the event of the mayor's resignation or recall, the remaining members of the city council shall choose his successor for the unexpired term, from their own number.

"Sec. 42. General Powers and Duties. The powers and duties of the mayor shall be such as are conferred upon him by this act, together with such others as are conferred by the city council in pursuance of the provisions of this act, and no others.

"Sec. 43. President of City Council. He shall be president of the city council and shall exercise all the powers conferred and perform all the duties imposed upon the presiding officer of the common council by the charter which are not inconsistent with this act. He shall appoint all standing and special committees of the city council. He shall be recognized as the official head of the city by the courts for the purpose of serving civil processes, by the Governor for the purposes of the military law, and for all ceremonial purposes.

"Sec. 44. Police and Military Powers. His power to take command of the police and to govern the city by proclamation during times of great public danger shall not be abridged or abrogated.

"Sec. 45. Designation to Judicial Vacancies. During the disability of any municipal judge or justice of the peace the mayor shall designate some properly qualified person to act during such disability.

"Sec. 46. Magisterial Powers. He shall have power to administer oaths and take affidavits.

"Sec. 47. Commissioner of Charities in Certain Cities. In cities where the mayor is authorized by charter to sit with the supervisors as a commissioner of charities, he shall continue so to act.

"Sec. 48. Removal by Governor. The power of the Governor to remove the mayor shall not be abridged.

"Sec. 49. No Judicial Powers; Mayor's Courts Abolished. The mayor shall have no judicial power. The mayor's Court of Special Sessions and all other mayor's courts are hereby abolished. The jurisdiction of the same shall be conferred by the city council upon some other municipal court.

"Sec. 50. Non-enumerated Functions. Such functions, not enumerated in this act, as are conferred upon the mayor of the city by charter or by the general laws of the state shall be exercised by the city manager unless some other provision shall be made by the city council.

"Sec. 51. Salary. The salary of the mayor shall be twice the salary, if any, received by any other member of the city council.

"Sec. 52. Acting Mayor. During the disability of the mayor, the functions of his office shall devolve upon some member of the city council designated by that body, who shall receive during such incumbency a pro rata of the excess over the alderman's salary which is allowed to the mayor under this act.

"ARTICLE VII.

"THE CITY MANAGER.

"Sec. 53. Administrative Head of Government. There shall be chosen by the city council an officer to be known as the city manager, who shall be the administrative head of the city government.

"Sec. 54. Official Oath and Bond. Before entering upon the duties of his office the city manager shall take the official oath required by law and shall execute a bond in favor of the city for the faithful performance of his duties in such sum as shall be determined upon by the city council.

"Sec. 55. Tenure of Office. The tenure of the city manager shall be at the pleasure of the city council.

"Sec. 56. Not to Be Interested. The city manager shall not be personally interested in any contracts to which the city is a party, for supplying the city with materials of any kind.

"Sec. 57. Duties: General. It shall be the duty of the city manager to see that within the city the laws of this state and the ordinances, resolutions and by-laws of the city council shall be faithfully executed. In addition to such functions as are enumerated in this act he shall exercise all other powers and perform all other duties conferred and imposed upon mayors of cities, unless other designation shall be made by this act or by act of the city council.

"Sec. 58. Recommendations and Reports. It shall be his duty to attend all meetings of, and to recommend to, the city council, from time to time, such measures as he shall deem necessary or expedient for it to adopt. He shall prepare business, and draw up resolutions and ordinances for adoption by the city council, and furnish them with any necessary information respecting any of the departments under his control.

"He shall, at such times as the city council shall so require, present reports from the several departments, and shall draw up an annual report which shall consolidate the special reports of the several departments. He shall be a member of the Board of Estimate and Apportionment and shall present to that body, annually, an itemized estimate of the financial needs of the several departments for the ensuing year.

"Sec. 59. Appointments. He shall appoint persons to fill all offices for which no other mode of appointment is provided. And no such appointment to or removal from such office shall be made without his consent.

"Sec. 60. Relation to Department Heads. He shall transmit to the heads of the several departments written notice of all acts of the city council relating to the duties of their departments, and he shall make designations of officers to perform duties ordered to be performed by the city council.

"Sec. 61. Signs Certain Documents. He shall sign such contracts, licenses and other public documents, on behalf of the city, as the city council may authorize and require.

"Sec. 62. Access to Public Records. He shall have access at all times to the books, vouchers and papers of any officer or employee of the city and shall have power to examine, under oath, any person connected therewith. It shall be his duty, either in person or by the aid of a competent expert, to know the manner in which the accounts of the city and the various boards are kept.

"Sec. 63. Signs Warrants of Arrest. He shall have power to sign warrants of arrest and to cause arrests for infraction, within the city, of the laws of the state and ordinances and other regulations of the city. He shall have general power to administer oaths and take affidavits.

"Sec. 64. May Revoke Licenses. He shall have power to revoke licenses pending the action of the city council.

"Sec. 65. Office Consolidated with City Clerk's in Certain Cities. In cities having a population of less than twenty thousand, according to the last preceding state enumeration, the office of city manager may be consolidated with that of city clerk, or other officer of similar functions.

"Sec. 66. Disability. During the disability of the city manager the city council shall designate some properly qualified person to execute the functions of the office.

"ARTICLE VIII.

"[Secs. 67 to 74 contain special provisions to obviate possible conflicts of the act with provisions of the special city charters.]

"ARTICLE IX.

"[Secs. 75 to 82 relate to certain special matters of local significance in regard to appointments.]

"ARTICLE X.

"THE DEPARTMENT OF EDUCATION.

"[By Secs. 83 to 94 the board of education is divested of its corporate character, and, so far as conditions permit, made a department of the general administration of the city. The board is appointed by the council.]

"ARTICLE XI.

"THE INITIATIVE AND REFERENDUM.

"[The provisions of this article, Secs. 95 to 99, are adapted from the charter of Berkeley, California(q. v.).]

"ARTICLE XII.

"[Miscellaneous provisions (Secs. 100 to 106).]

"B. OHIO STATUTE.

[Laws of 1913, p. 767, *et seq.* Applicable to any city in Ohio by referendum.]

"ARTICLE IV.

"Sec. 8. City Manager. The council shall appoint a city manager who shall be the administrative head of the municipal government under the direction and supervision of the council and who shall hold office at the pleasure of the council.

"Sec. 9. Duties of City Manager. The duties of

the city manager shall be: (a) to see that the laws and ordinances are faithfully executed; (b) to attend all meetings of the council at which his attendance may be required by that body; (c) to recommend for adoption to the council such measures as he may deem necessary or expedient; (d) to appoint all officers and employees in the classified service of the municipality, subject to the provisions of this act,* and of the civil service law; (e) to prepare and submit to the council such reports as may be required by that body, or as he may deem advisable to submit; (f) to keep the council fully advised of the financial condition of the municipality and its future needs; (g) to prepare and submit to the council a tentative budget for the next fiscal year; (h) and to perform such other duties as the council may determine by ordinance or resolution.

"Sec. 10. Salary of City Manager. The city manager shall receive such salary as may be fixed by the council; and before entering upon the duties of this office he shall take the official oath required by this act and shall execute a bond in favor of the municipality for the faithful performance of his duties in such sum as may be fixed by the council."

* The council appoints the auditor, clerk, treasurer and solicitor.

"C. VIRGINIA STATUTE.

[An act of the legislature, approved Mar. 13, 1914, applicable to every city having less than 100,000 inhabitants, when adopted at a special election called upon petition of 25 per cent. of the electors qualified to vote at the last preceding municipal election.]

"I. GENERAL COUNCILMANIC PLAN.

"*Governing Body:*
    "*Title:*   Council.
    "*Term of Office:* Four years.
    "*Number:*   Population less than 10,000 — three * or five elected at large.
                          Population 10,000 to 20,000 — three, five or seven elected at large or by wards.*
                          Population 20,000 to 30,000—three, five, seven or nine, to be elected at large or by wards.
                          Population over 30,000—three,* five, seven, nine or eleven, to be elected at large or by wards.

* [*See* footnote on p. 193.]

"Any city operating under this plan, or any town, may appoint any person who is a qualified resident of such city or town, to be known as 'city manager' and to perform such duties as the council may require of him and for such compensation as they may allow. Such officer is subject to removal by the council at any time.

"II. MODIFIED COMMISSION PLAN.

"*Governing Body:*
    "*Title:*   Council.
    "*Term of Office:*   Four years.
    "*Number:*   Three,* or five, elected at large.

"*Appointments:*
    "*Manner:*   By the council, subject to removal by that body at any time except as especially provided by law.

"III. CITY MANAGER PLAN.

"*Governing Body:*
    "*Number:*   Population less than 10,000—three * or five, elected at large.
    Population over 10,000—

* [*See* footnote on p. 193.]

five * to eleven.

"*Term of Office:* Four years.

"*City Manager:*

"*Administrative and executive powers.* The administrative and executive powers of the city, including the power of appointment of officers and employees, are vested in an official to be known as the city manager, who shall be appointed by the council at its first meeting, or as soon thereafter as practicable, and hold office during the pleasure of the council; he shall receive such compensation as shall be fixed by the council by ordinance.

"*General Duties of the City Manager.*

"1. The city manager shall see that within the city the laws, ordinances, resolutions and by-laws of the council are faithfully executed.

"2. Attend all meetings of the council, and recommend for adoption such measures as he shall deem expedient.

"3. Make reports to the council from time to time upon the affairs of the city; keep the council fully advised of the city's financial condition, and its future financial needs.

"4. Prepare and submit to the council a tentative budget for the next fiscal year.

"5. He shall perform such other duties as may be

* [*See* footnote on p. 193.]

prescribed by the council not in conflict with the foregoing, and shall be bonded as the council may deem necessary.

(*See also* "Appointments.")

"*Appointments:*
   "*Manner:* By the city manager, subject to removal by him (except those in the financial, legal and judicial departments and the clerical and other attendants of the council).

"Under this plan the council selects one of its own number to preside over its meetings, who becomes, thereupon, *ex-officio* mayor.

"PROVISIONS APPLICABLE TO EACH PLAN.

"*Elections:*
   "The general state law providing for partisan elections only, applies.

"*Initiative:*
   "No provisions.

"*Referendum:*
   "No provisions.

"Recall:

"No provisions."

* The adoption of a particular plan of government is coupled on the ballot with propositions fixing the number and compensation of councilmen for the particular city and, in some cases, determining whether election shall be by wards or at large.

"Under this plan, the council selects one of its own number to preside over its meetings, with the title of mayor, and assigns each one of its members to particular administrative duties."

CHAPTER XII

RESULTS

I believe that one of the greatest moral services, even if one of the most unpleasant duties, of the public-spirited citizen is to watch continuously the conduct of the public officials who represent him.

HENRY CROSBY EMERY

It is a majestic outlook to view the accomplishments of municipal revolutions of the past years. A certain poetic fitness of things seems to pervade these concentrated efforts, courageous, intelligent, humanitarian efforts, to make city life a thing of order and system and clean-minded business—an evidence even of that sterner phase of a practical religion of true citizenship; a religion which elevates industrious attention to the duties of a citizen as one of the primal duties of an urban resident.

Fine fruits of this new religion have been born in this forward movement appearing in the guise of the city manager' plan. From the very nature of things, it is the report of progress of a thing newly born. The facts should be left to speak for themselves; but the prospects they predict are rare visions of a new order about to come into the fullness of its own excellent state.

When the new commission under the city manager charter entered upon its duties in Springfield, Ohio, it was faced by a floating indebtedness of $123,000. This had been accumulating for years; it was heritage of past evils. After six months of progressive work it is definitely expected to reduce this to $55,000 or $60,000 at the end of the first year and to totally eliminate the entire floating indebtedness by the end of the second year. And as a means to do all this, the first competent step was the employment of highly expert accountants of a famous firm to install a model accounting system, entirely uniform and unified, placing the city upon the bedrock basis of assets and resources. The cost of the installation of such a system is $5,000, but the expense will be entirely saved and more by the results obtained on the investigation and the installation of the system. For instance, the water department had been reputed to be a fabled gold mine returning in profit apparently $60,000 to $75,000 to the city yearly. Under the accounting system just installed a rude blow was dealt to this bonanza. The ridiculous situation was discovered that the amateur financiers of prior administrations had neglected to charge depreciation, interest on investment and a number of other vital items; the actual profits were found to be of another degree entirely than those which had been accredited to the department for years.

From now on public buildings, schools and other places of similar character will have to pay for the water furnished to them; they will no longer be allowed to act the parasite upon another department.

By a system of economy and the application of a business organization to the department, the proper charging of water rentals, as well as other means, will restore somewhat this decrease in the profits of the water department. But the instance tellingly illustrates the fallacies upon which the old government was based. Consider the character of business judgment which ran a $45,000,000 corporation and permitted the condition of things set forth above!

One of the first steps taken in Springfield was a reduction of the police and fire department force because there was no money with which to pay them, and the services in some instances were not vital. For instance, a fire engine house also was closed and the members of the companies retired from the force, but placed upon the civil service list at the head so that in case of vacancies they could be reinstated first of all.

A radical change was made in the amount of labor and the character of labor on the part of the city employees. For the first time in the history of a town the hours of seven o'clock A. M. to twelve o'clock noon and from one o'clock P. M. until five o'clock P. M. were rigidly observed. And during those hours the officials attended to the city's business and they did not occupy their time with a great deal of political discussion, "wire-pulling" or other means of wasting the hours for which someone else pays. Merit alone determines the retention of an official and every official in the city government has been and is being measured according to that standard. Some have not been able to measure up to the ordinary business requirements and have been asked to secure other employment. This process cannot be over within the first six months nor perhaps will ever be over. A radical change was made in one instance: the fire chief had not been requested in former days to stay on duty in the Central Engine House continually, but now he lives there and makes that his headquarters. Rapid strides are being made in the motorizing of the entire fire department, which will effect a vast economy in current expense.

Experts alone are employed. The auditor is a former state examiner and the auditing department is conducted in a highly commendable manner, preventing a practice which is said to have been quite frequent in the old administration, of paying bills more than once.

The streets are now repaired and cleaned under the direct supervision of the chief engineer. He has in constant mind the very best permanent, scientific repairs, and with the aid of a street cleaning department, which has been entirely motorized, he can keep the streets in excellent condition. The motor truck is handled and loaded by three men and when it starts out along a street to clean it the vehicle never stops, but is loaded while being moved. The saving in this item will pay for the motorizing feature in a year. The repair of the streets is done by the city now; and the cuts, fills, and other changes are so performed by the city. If there is any defective street, a telephone message to the city manager will secure immediate action in the following manner, which is in vital contrast to the old method of delay. Upon receipt of the telephone message, the city manager will send a written order to the proper department to see that the matter is attended to, and this job must be reported back to him when done. The work is not performed as soon as the official can get ready, upon his own statement, but is performed at once. If it is a matter demanding the promptest attention, the order is telephoned to the department by the city manager and the written request follows.

The secretary to the city manager, a trained newspaper man, has been acting as purchasing agent, and to him come the questions of that position; it is estimated that he will save the city $8,000 during the first year.

The health department has been reformed. The health director and his assistant are both doctors of excellent training who keep the same office hours of seven o'clock to five o'clock as the rest of the city officials, and in addition are subject to call for night work in emergency cases. The dairy and food commissioners, the sanitary marshal, the pathologist, are all abolished. The position of the pathologist is now occupied by the health director or his assistant who have had a laboratory fitted up for them.

The new plan is followed in the proper financing of the bond issues in issuing of bonds to cover the actual cost of improvements rather than the estimated cost. The old plan of issuing on estimated cost and then having to rebate when actual cost was found out, involved a loss, practically, of the interest on the excess of bonds, and the reforms in this particular will save $50,000 to $75,000. Along the line of bond issues for street improvements, it is interesting to note that now no underground street improvements will be permitted after a street has once been laid.

Fifty thousand dollars will be saved this year in running expenses approximately, and the tax rate will be reduced somewhat despite the increased scope of activities.

The city manager requires a report from the manager of every department each day. This report includes many items, among them, the number of men at work, hours of labor, the amount of wages, and other necessary items to show the cost of what they are producing. Every two weeks all heads of departments have a conference with the city manager.

A new gas franchise was entered into for a ten-year period which, it is estimated, will save the city $75,000.

In Dayton, Ohio, of course, the problems to be met were different, and the scope of the reform was much vaster. The following report of Mr. Waite, city manager of Dayton, as published by The Dayton Bureau of Research, is given entirely as a statement of what the new administration considers it has become through the city manager plan. This report covers the period of the first six months of the operation of the plan.

Office of the Manager

"*Staff Conferences.*—Regular conferences with the heads of departments are held, where all important matters are considered and departmental cooperation has been developed, and the programs and activities of each department are discussed and planned.

"*Expenditures Limited by Income.*—In planning the expenditures of the year, appropriations were limited to estimated revenues, and expenditures are being kept within the cash receipts. The old deficit of $125,000 will be reduced rather than added to. The issuance of bonds to meet current expenses has not been resorted to.

"*An Eight-hour Day.*—Payrolls are not now passed unless a time sheet has been kept showing the number of hours worked by each employee. In this connection the number of hours has been reduced from 10 to 8, at the same pay, and office employees are now required to work a full eight hours.

"*Grade Elimination.*—Five thousand dollars has been appropriated with which to prepare grade elimination plans, providing those now being secured by the railroads are unsatisfactory. This contemplates the elevation of the joint tracks through the center of the city, which must be done before the other crossings can be considered.

"*Building Code.*—Arranged for the drafting of an entire building code for the city to be ready January 1, 1915, and without cost to the city.

"*Better Street Car Service.*—Secured from the railways, switchmen for the downtown intersections during rush hours. The companies are also considering a complete re-routing to reduce the downtown congestion.

"*A Civic Plan Board.*—There has been appointed a Civic Plan Board to investigate the subject of city planning and report a program of city development, including a civic center for the location of public buildings.

"*Civic Music.*—Amateur and professional musicians have been interested in securing high-grade music at more popular prices. As a result, there has been arranged a high-class symphony program for the coming winter, and half of the seating capacity has been sold in season tickets.

"*Renaming and Renumbering Streets.*—A commission has been appointed to recommend a plan for renaming and renumbering certain streets.

"*Life-saving Equipment.*—Through the generosity of a citizen life-saving equipment has been secured for stations along the river and one fireman sent to the U. S. Life Saving Station at Cleveland to study rescue and resuscitation, and a life-saving crew has been organized in the Division of Fire.

"*Crossing Blockades.*—Since the first of the year, every crossing blockade has been reported to the manager's office, and a report of the cause received from the railway. A gradual reduction in delays has resulted, and material betterment in service secured.

"*Civic Workers' League.*—The women of the city were interested in forming such an organization to aid in keeping the city clean, and have offered prizes to the school districts showing the greatest improvement.

"*Traffic Rules.*—A commission has been appointed to revise the present traffic regulations and present to the Commission a code which will meet the requirements of a growing city.

"*Additional Water.*—Arrangements have been entered into with a firm of consulting engineers to present plans for an adequate water extension for a population of over 200,000.

"*Garbage Removal.*—Plans have been secured for a disposal plant and the equipment necessary to care for all garbage and other refuse of the city, considering its growth for twenty years.

"*Sewers.*—Both the storm and sanitary sewer systems are inadequate for the present needs of the city and funds have been voted with which to design a complete sewer system, and all sewers laid in the future will be in accordance with this plan.

"*The Park System.*—Several years ago Mr. Olmstead prepared a comprehensive park plan for Dayton. This is being published and as a first step in carrying out the scheme, the condemnation of the Orth, Herman Avenue and other dumps has been recommended.

"*Petty Offenders.*—The city spends thousands of dollars each year caring for petty offenders, drunkards, etc., many of them 'repeaters.' Without cost to the city, an investigation is being made which, it is hoped, will indicate to the Welfare Department the most humane treatment of these persons.

DEPARTMENT OF LAW

"*Settlement of Complaints.*—The prosecutor's office is disposing of all cases without arrests wherever possible. Approximately 100 questions concerning rents, family troubles, petty quarrels are now settled weekly without court publicity.

"*Loan Shark Campaign.*—In conjunction with the Legal Aid Bureau several successful actions have been brought against loan agents, resulting in wholesale settlements at legal rates of interest.

"Parole of Workhouse Prisoners.—In many worthy cases workhouse prisoners have been paroled and placed on probation, and work secured for them. There is need for further development of this feature.

"Mail Order Frauds.—The prosecutor coöperated with other public officers in securing evidence of mail order fraud, and one case has been turned over to the United States' authorities.

"Home Rule.—The most sweeping decision in favor of a liberal interpretation of the home rule amendment was secured from the Supreme Court in the decision upholding the legality of local civil service laws.

"General Statement.—Operating under a new charter has made it necessary to refer to the Legal Department all new activities and an immense amount of work has been performed by them of value not only to the city in general but affecting every home rule municipality.

DEPARTMENT OF PUBLIC SERVICE

Office of the Director

"A Salary Saving of $2,700.—A reduction in the number of office positions in the department has made possible a saving of $2,700 for the year.

"*Expediting Public Work.*—By borrowing on the credit of uncollected assessments contractors are being paid promptly, and work rushed with a resulting lower cost. Formerly contractors did work and were paid only as assessments were actually collected.

"*Permits Simplified.*—All permits are now issued from one office, on a uniform form, and the amount collected recorded on a cash register. At the same time the machine stamps the permit as legal, and indicates the amount paid.

"*Future Refuse Disposal.*—A report has been secured from the sanitary engineers, Hering and Gregory of New York, as to the future needs of the city for garbage and refuse collection and disposal.

Division of Engineering

"*Investigation of Sewers.*—A complete topographical study of the city has been planned and an investigation of the condition of all storm and sanitary sewers. The plan will provide for future development and for a sewage disposal plant to be ready if such is ordered by the State Board of Health. All future sewer construction will be made to this plan.

"*Efficient Street Inspection.* — The inspection

service on contracts has been completely reorganized and contractors required to conform rigidly to specifications. The result will be a better grade of street pavement in the future.

"*Island Park Bridge.*—By using the span of the Webster Street Bridge, the Island Park Bridge was restored at the low cost of $4,000.

"*$12,000 Saved on Valley Street Bridge.*—Permission was secured from the State Board of Public Works to fill and pave Valley Street across the Miami and Erie Canal instead of building a lift bridge, for which money had been appropriated. Twelve thousand dollars was turned back into the sinking fund.

Division of Streets

"*Street Oiling.*—Twenty oiling districts for gravel streets have been created, and all streets were properly prepared and cleaned before being oiled.

"*Refuse Collection.*—The collection of rubbish and ashes discontinued last year has been resumed. The streets and alleys of the city have been cleaned up and the wagons have been routed so that monthly service is rendered to all sections of the city alike.

"*Garbage Collection.*—It has been arranged to give the householders regular garbage collection service weekly. That adequate service may be supplied with the funds available, it has been asked that only garbage be put in the cans, and then the cans be placed of easy access to the collectors.

"*Dead Animals.*—The collection of dead animals, which formerly cost the city $1,700 a year, is now being done free. Complaints should be telephoned to Main 376.

"*Street Flushing.*—The downtown streets are being flushed once a week. This replaces sprinkling and will be assessed on the abutting property. It is hoped that the results will next year justify increasing the flushing to all paved streets.

"*For Cleaner Streets.*—In addition to enlarging the area cleaned by 'White Wings,' all paved streets are being swept once in ten days by large power brooms. Sixty refuse cans have been placed on the main thoroughfares, and a clean-up gang been placed on the downtown streets on Saturday night at midnight, in order that the streets may be clean Sunday.

"*Street Repairs.*—Street repairs except for a balance of $12 000 remaining from bonds issued before 1914, are now being made from current revenues. Where asphalt streets are in too bad a condition they are being repaired with tar macadam at a reduced cost.

"*Service Cuts.*—All plumbers' cuts except for those issued prior to May 1 are now being made by this division and the cost paid by the person having the work done. This insures a more satisfactory restoration of the street surface.

"*Improvement of Dumps.*—Have leveled off and graded Washington Street dump and part of Herman Avenue dump, as well as removed a large amount of brick, stone and débris from the vacant lots used as gardens.

Division of Water

"*Increased Water Pressure.*—Since June 4 a pressure of 70 pounds instead of the normal 40 to 60 pounds has been maintained during all periods of heavy consumption. The distribution system, however, is so inadequate that even this pressure will not supply all sections. On account of reserve for fire service it is inadvisable to increase beyond 70 pounds.

"*Additional Water Supply.*—A temporary supply of about 7,000,000 gallons of water per day has been made available at Tate's Hill. This has provided for the increased demand which has frequently exceeded 16,000,000 gallons per day. During fires the consumption has exceeded the rate of

30,000,000 gallons per day. Work on the permanent additional supply from Tate's Hill is being actively pushed and will be completed this fall.

Improved Pumping.—The pumping machinery has been completely overhauled, and the slippage greatly reduced in two of the three units. Two pumps are now used for normal service, leaving the third for peak loads, fires, sprinkling hours, wash days, etc. The city is paid for only one-half of the water pumped as shown by piston displacement measurements. This waste is gradually being reduced by reducing slippage, using better meters, eliminating leaks, etc.

"*Plans for Water Improvements.*—A firm of consulting engineers are making an investigation of the entire water situation, including supply, pumping and distribution, and a report will shortly be made with recommendations for comprehensive improvements. These recommendations will consider the demands of a population of over 200,000.

"*Dayton View Supply.*—High pressure pumps have been installed at Keowee Street station so that the tank in Dayton View can be filled without putting on fire pressure. The territory served by the tank has been materially extended, securing a broader and more equal distribution of benefits.

"*Reduced Coal Consumption.*—In spite of the increased quantity of water pumped, the amount of coal burned has decreased. This is due to the improvements made in the pumping equipment and to the fact that all coal delivered is tested for ash and heating value, and required to conform to contract specifications.

"*Meter Repairs.*—Meter repairs now cost over $12,000 a year. Records have been installed to show the repair cost of each meter in order that the most durable type may be learned and purchased in the future.

"*A Water Works' Superintendent.*—A superintendent has been appointed, placing the whole division under one executive head instead of three. The position of cashier and office manager will be abolished August 1.

Division of Public Lands and Buildings

"*Municipal Garage.*—All motor repairs and adjustments are now being made at the motor garage at a saving of several thousand dollars a year. The garage also acts as a clearing house, securing greater service from the motor equipment of the city. All city cars are now numbered and labeled. This facilitates the keeping of cost records over the operation and repair of each car, and prevents 'joy riding' after hours.

"*Alterations in City Building.*—By making alterations in the city building, quarters were provided for the three judges of the municipal court, the city manager, purchasing agent, and city sealer. This saves a once proposed expenditure of over $2,000 a year for rent.

"*Savings on Heat.*—By heating the city building with purchased steam two old boilers and the service of two engineers were dispensed with, effecting a saving of $700 per year.

DEPARTMENT OF PUBLIC WELFARE

Division of Health

"*Full Time Health Officer.*—Provided a health officer on full time, the first in the history of the city. Also increased the force of full time food and dairy inspectors, and rearranged the work so as to secure larger services from each employee.

"*New Quarters.*—Removed the health offices from a residence to a modern office building, paying approximately the same rent, and giving space to two other departments formerly paying rent.

"*Reorganization of Health Work.*—Reorganized the entire division of health and installed complete up-to-the-minute records, insuring systematic work, increased efficiency, and adequate control of health problems. The work of the sanitary police has been doubled, and the force reduced.

"*Public Health Nursing.*—With the coöperation and the help of the Visiting Nurses' Association and the Tuberculosis Society, brought under one management and single control all public health nursing.

"*Vacant Property.*—Ordinances were secured regulating dumping grounds in the city, and the creation of insanitary, disease-breeding centers by indiscriminate dumping is being prevented. Owners are also required to cut weeds on vacant lots.

"*Insanitary Conditions.*—Enforced the laws and ordinances against insanitary dwellings and premises, open manure boxes, throwing of garbage and vegetable matter in alleys, on levees and vacant lots, to insure better health conditions in the city.

"*A Lower Baby Death Rate.*—The death rate for infants for June, 1914, was only one-half that of any June for three years previous. This low death rate has been secured by successfully controlling threatened epidemics of small-pox and diphtheria; by an anti-fly campaign conducted through every public and parochial school; and by the inauguration of baby welfare work. Three weekly baby clinics and four certified milk stations have been established as well as a system of postnatal visiting to mothers.

"*Free Public Clinics.*—Free eye, ear and throat clinics have been established at the two hospitals, and a tuberculosis and a general clinic at the Welfare Department.

Division of Parks

"*McCabe's Park.*—McCabe's Park has been opened to the public; a storm sewer built for less than two-thirds the appropriation and a satisfactory lighting system installed.

"*McKinley Park.*—A running track has been built at McKinley Park; filled in the low places and made a baseball diamond; terraced the southwest corner where four additional tennis courts have been built, and with the coöperation of Service Department, are changing and widening River Street near Forest Avenue, making it safe to pedestrians.

"*Island Park.*—Cleaned up Island Park (formerly White City) from the ravages of the flood of last year; filled up the unused swimming pool; built a wading pool for small children; tore away the old moving-picture theater and out of the lumber built two toilet rooms; dug a channel with workhouse labor connecting the Miami River with the lagoon at the east side of the park, turning the park into an island; rehabilitated and repainted all buildings on the ground; rebuilt the roads and planted shrubbery and flowers; put in three bubbling fountains; installed an additional lighting system which lights up the entire island and the beach, making bathing possible in the evenings; reinforced the pillars and girders of the dancing pavilion, making it safe; resurfaced the dancing floor, and installed new awnings on the building.

"With the splendid coöperation of the Dayton Canoe Club opened the park with a water carnival which was witnessed by more than 10,000 people. The number of citizens daily enjoying the privileges of this park are proof sufficient of the needs of public amusement.

"*Community Gardens.*—Plowed and prepared in coöperation with the Dayton Playgrounds and Gardens Association six community gardens on which about 75 families are cultivating vegetables; plowed and prepared 22 experimental gardens for the cultivation of vegetables by hundreds of children under the direction of an expert gardener; plowed and prepared 339 vacant lot gardens on which as many families are raising vegetables; cleaned up and leveled up and prepared for the children, a dozen additional playgrounds.

Division of Recreation

"*Reorganization of Playground Work.*—Secured with the equal assistance of the Dayton Playgrounds and Gardens Association the services of an expert in recreation who made a study of Dayton's needs in this field. At the suggestion of this investigator and with the coöperation of the Public School Board and the Dayton Playgrounds and Gardens Association, an advisory board of recreation was created under whose management all the public recreation of the city is being conducted, unifying the work and doubling its scope by more than one hundred per cent.

"*Number of Playgrounds Doubled.*—Playgrounds have been opened in every section of the city, with daily supervision by trained play-supervisors, all under the direction of the superintendent of recreation. There are now 28 playgrounds in Dayton as against 14 or 15 last year, the largest number ever reached.

"*New Equipment Secured.*—Extra back-stops for baseball have been built by the department and erected on vacant lots in addition to those erected on regular supervised playgrounds, making about 35 play-centers for children and young people. At Island Park new floats were built; new bathing suits purchased; ten new steel boats bought; the beach widened and sanded for bathers; a complete life-saving station established with a fast gasoline launch, thoroughly equipped for saving life and manned by a trained life-saver, from 8:00 A. M. to 12:00 midnight. New tables for family dinners were built and 100 park benches added. Players' benches have been placed on all ball grounds and the playing fields carefully lined.

"*Play Tournaments.*—A large number of tournaments have been inaugurated for the summer which will create an unusual interest in all sorts of play —such as marbles, kite-flying, baseball, quoits, swimming, athletic contests, as well as doll dressing, jackstones, volley ball and sand models for the girls.

Division of Correction

"*Workhouse Overhauled.*—The workhouse has been completely overhauled; a fresh coat of paint and whitewash was given the entire interior; broken windows replaced; new cots, blankets and sheeting purchased; and the entire kitchen refitted with modern equipment to replace the lard cans, etc., formerly used as cooking pots. The cistern has been thoroughly cleaned, disinfected and put into use, cutting the soap cost in half. All prisoners fitted out with new clothing and many with new shoes. New fire hose has been bought to insure increased fire protection. A half-dozen sewing machines have been furnished by the Davis Company for the use of the women, who are making towels and bed clothing, and repairing men's clothing.

"*The Police Station.*—The police station prison has been transferred to the care of the Division of Corrections, and hot rations from the workhouse kitchen furnished prisoners in place of hard-tack and bologna.

"*Cost Records Installed.*—A complete system of cost and service records to show the daily cost of maintaining prisoners has been installed, and the office procedure brought up to date.

"*Workhouse Labor.*—In the interest of health and discipline, prisoners have been put at outside work whenever possible, and on tasks which would otherwise have gone undone. Over 1,000 days' labor has been done at the following places: Island Park, city garden, Tate's Hill, garbage station, McCabe's Park, Bomberger Park, city clean-up day,

Edgemont playground. Workhouse men also attend daily bridge flower boxes on Main and Warren Streets.

"*Municipal Lodging House Established.*—A municipal lodging house was temporarily established through the courtesy of the Burkhardt Packing Company, who gave free use of a building on Market Street. The superintendent of corrections managed this new feature of relief work, taking care of 1,852 lodgers. These lodgers were required to give a half-day's labor, removing snow, leveling dumps, etc., etc.

"*The City Garden.*—A city garden covering two acres has been planted by prisoners, with 18 bushels of potatoes, 2,000 cabbage plants, 800 tomato plants, besides beans, sweet corn, etc. This garden has furnished all the vegetables for the workhouse.

Division of Legal Aid

"*Free Legal Advice.*—A Division of Legal Aid was established in the Department of Welfare, the second of its kind under city control in this country. It has been unusually effective in protecting the weak, and in four months of operation has handled over 300 applications, most of which were claims for wages; installment difficulties and loan shark extortions. Over two-thirds of these were disposed of without legal action. Any person capable of paying is referred to private counsel. The maintenance of the division will cost less than $625 for the year.

Division of Charities

"City Infirmary Abolished.—The city infirmary was abolished February 1 and all outdoor relief put under the administration of the Associated Charities, thus unifying the work, increasing its efficiency and avoiding duplication of service. This field is being covered at less than one-half the cost formerly incurred by the city infirmary as conducted with a superintendent, an assistant, clerk and janitor.

Department of Public Safety

"Investigation of Fire and Police Service.—At no cost to the city the services of Mr. Clement Driscoll, ex-Deputy Police Commissioner of New York, were secured to study safety conditions. This report is now being prepared and will deal particularly with the redistribution of fire apparatus for added protection.

Division of Police

"*More Police.*—Seven additional patrolmen were provided for in the budget of 1914, and were appointed early in the year.

"*Women Probation Officers.*—Two women probation officers have been provided to care for girls and women requiring correctional measures, or in need of personal and sympathetic advice.

"*School for Police.*—To increase the effectiveness of the police force regular meetings are being held where the officers are schooled in police methods; departmental coöperation; ordinances pertaining to public health, service, etc. For the first time in the department weekly practice is being held in target shooting, with classification according to scores.

"*Uniforms and Drill.*—Semi-military uniforms have been secured for all officers, and service insignias will shortly be provided. Police drills are now being held to improve appearance and discipline.

"*Traffic Rules.*—Traffic rules have been amended and a rigid enforcement ordered.

Division of Fire

"*Fire Prevention.*—An inspection has been made of every building in the city to acquaint at least one fireman in each district with all interior constructions. In addition fire hazards were abated, and where orders for the removal of material or for changes in building conditions were given, re-inspections were made.

"*Service Tests.*—With a view to decreasing the time necessary to get into active service at fires, practice tests have been made on running lines, hoisting aerials, ladder mounting, etc. At the try-out before the fire underwriters, prizes for the most efficient men and companies were awarded by the Dayton Bicycle Club.

"*Motor Apparatus.*—Since it has been thought impractical to completely motorize the department at once, and would necessitate selling present apparatus for less than its value, only half of the money available for motor apparatus will be used. Fifty thousand dollars has been returned to the sinking fund."

This record of accomplishments is fraught with a great hope—the hope of rejuvenation of American municipal governments and the elevation of their administration to a unique place. The work is necessarily slow, laborious, and one calling for great tact and business judgment; that the administrators are displaying these qualities the achievements enumerated heretofore are ample testimonials.

CHAPTER XIII

VARIOUS POINTS OF VIEW

Where there is no counsel, purposes are disappointed;
But in the multitude of counsellors they are established.
                                                A PROVERB

The following report is an interesting verdict rendered by a jury of men whose personnel guarantees its thoroughness and impartiality. The discussion is as follows:

"SUPPLEMENTARY REPORT.
SUBMITTED AT THE TORONTO MEETING OF THE NATIONAL MUNICIPAL LEAGUE, NOVEMBER, 1913.

"Instead of 3,894,173 as in 1911, commission government now rules a population of 7,086,225 and the number of towns and cities under this form has increased from 93 to 300.

"The Des Moines charter is still the standard.

"Nine cities have followed the Grand Junction (Colo.) variation which provides the preferential ballot. The device has proven workable and economical and the extension of its use deserves encouragement.

"The recent city manager variation, hereinafter described, embodies the first significant change in structure.

"One much mooted question has always been whether commissioners should be elected for specific posts (as in Lynn, Mass.) or on a general ticket with power to divide the departments among themselves after election (as in Galveston and Des Moines). The tendency of charter makers since 1911 is toward the Lynn system. The Kansas law has been amended after a trial of the Des Moines plan and the Lynn plan substituted.

"The argument for the original general ticket plan is based on the grounds that the people will in either case elect on issues of representation rather than on issues of the technical fitness of candidates, and that in such case the commission by intensive close-hand investigation of the experience and ability of its members can make best use of the material available. Moreover, election to specific office tends to create five city governments instead of one, diminishes the influence and control of the commission over its individual members and thus interferes with the 'unification of powers.'

"Advocates of the 'specific-office' plan point out that candidates are entitled to know what their positions will be in the government and the voters, too, are entitled to know what department a given candidate, if successful, will direct. A candidate may not desire to run unless a certain department is to be his and the voter may willingly vote for a man as candidate for one department but not for another department.

"A majority of your committee believes that neither solution is as sound as that offered by the commission manager plan in which the whole question disappears (see '6' below).

"THE COMMISSION MANAGER VARIATION

"*Definition of the commission manager plan.*—A single elective board (commission) representative, supervisory and legislative in function, the members giving only part time to municipal work and receiving nominal salaries or none. An appointive chief executive (city manager) hired by the board from anywhere in the country and holding office at the pleasure of the board. The manager appoints and controls the remaining city employees, subject to adequate civil service provisions.

"*History.*—The first commission manager charter was presented to the legislature of New York in 1911 by the Lockport Board of Trade and widely commented upon as 'the Lockport plan.' It failed of passage in the Legislature.

"In 1912 it was adopted by the South Carolina Legislature in a special act for the city of Sumter (population, 8,109), and subsequently adopted by that city, going into effect January 1, 1913, and thereafter known as the Sumter plan.

"In 1913 it was adopted by Hickory, N. C. (population, 3,176); and Morganton, N. C. (population, 2,712); Dayton, Ohio (population, 116,577); Springfield, Ohio (population, 46,921); La Grande, Ore. (population, 4,843); Phœnix, Ariz. (population, 11,134); Morris, Minn. (population, 1,885). Adopted as one of three plans in a general optional law by the Ohio Legislature, applicable to any city.

"It was also submitted, unsuccessfully, in Elyria and Youngstown, Ohio.

"The Lockport draft remains at present the model and the Springfield charter is the best thus far put into effect.

"*Comments.*—The swift development of popularity for the city manager idea insures a wide and thorough trial of the plan and its rapid spread may be confidently predicted.

"This variation has both of the great basic

merits which our earlier report ascribed to the original commission plan, namely, the 'unification of powers' and 'the short ballot.'

"At this point the committee divides.

"MAJORITY REPORT

"By Charles A. Beard, Clinton Rogers Woodruff, William Bennett Munro and Richard S. Childs.

"The city manager feature is a valuable addition to the commission plan, and we recommend to charter makers serious consideration of the inclusion of this feature in new commission government charters. Its advantages are:

"1. It creates a single-headed administrative establishment instead of the five separate administrative establishments seen in the Des Moines plan. This administrative unity makes for harmony between municipal departments, since all are subject to a common head.

"2. The commission manager plan permits expertness in administration at the point where it is most valuable, namely, at the head.

"3. It permits comparative permanence in the office of the chief executive, whereas in all plans involving elective executives, long tenures are rare.

"a. This permanence tends to rid us of amateur and transient executives and to substitute experienced experts.

"b. This permanence gives to the administrative establishment the superior stability and continuity of personnel and policies which is a necessary precedent to solid and enduring administrative reforms.

"c. This permanence makes more feasible the consideration and carrying out of far-sighted projects extending over long terms of years.

"d. This permanence makes it worth while for the executives to educate themselves seriously in municipal affairs, in the assurance that such education will be useful over a long period and in more than one city.

"4. The commission manager plan permits the chief executives to migrate from city to city, inasmuch as the city manager is not to be necessarily a resident of the city at the time of his appointment, and thus an experienced man can be summoned at advanced salary from a similar post in another city.

"a. This exchangeability opens up a splendid new profession, that of 'city managership.'

"b. This exchangeability provides an ideal vehicle for the interchange of experience among the cities.

"5. The commission manager plan, while giving a single-headed administration, abolishes the one-man power seen in the old mayor-and-council plan. The manager has no independence and the city need not suffer from his personal whims or prejudices, since he is subject to instant correction, or even discharge, by the commission. Likewise, in the commission, each member's individual whims or prejudices are safely submerged and averaged in the combined judgment of the whole commission, since no member exerts any authority in the municipal government save as one voting member of the commission.

"a. This abolition of one-man power makes safer the free-handed extension of municipal powers and operations unhampered by checks and balances and red tape.

"b. More discretion can be left to administrative officers to establish rulings as they go along, since they are subject to continuous control and the ultimate appeal of dissatisfied citizens is to the fairness and intelligence of a group (the commission) rather than to a single and possibly opinionated man (an elective mayor). Inversely, laws and ordinances can be simpler, thus reducing the field of legal interpretation and bringing municipal business nearer to the simplicity, flexibility and straightforwardness of private business.

"6. The commission manager plan abandons all attempts to choose administrators by popular election. This is desirable because:

"a. It is as difficult for the people to gauge executive and administrative ability in candidates as to estimate the professional worth of engineers or attorneys. As stated under No. 13 in our 1911 report, such tasks are not properly popular functions.

"b. By removing all requirements of technical or administrative ability in elective officers, it broadens the field of popular choice and leaves the people free to follow their instinct which is to choose candidates primarily with reference to their representative character only. Laboring men, for instance, can then freely elect their own men to the commission, and there is no requirement (as in the Des Moines charter) that these representatives shall, despite their inexperience in managing large affairs, be given the active personal management of a more or less technical municipal department.

"7. The commission manager plan leaves the lines of responsibility unmistakably clear, avoiding the confusion in the Des Moines plan between the responsibility of the individual commissioners and that of the commission as a whole.

"8. It provides basis for better discipline and harmony, inasmuch as the city manager cannot safely be at odds with the commission, as can the Des Moines commissioners in their capacity as department heads, or the mayor with the council in the mayor-and-council plan.

"9. It is better adapted for large cities than the Des Moines plan.

"Large cities should have more than five members in their commission to avoid overloading the members with work and responsibility, and to avoid conferring too much legislative power per individual member.

"Unlike the Des Moines plan, the commission manager plan permits such enlarged commissions, and so opens the way to the broader and more diversified representation which large cities need.

"10. In very small cities, by providing the services of one well-paid manager instead of five or three paid commissioners, it makes possible economy in salaries and overhead expenses.

"11. It permits ward elections or proportional representation as the Des Moines plan does not. One or the other of these is likely to prove desirable in very large cities to preserve a district size that will not be so big that the cost and difficulty of effective canvassing will balk independent candidacies, thereby giving a monopoly of hopeful nominations to permanent political machines (see No. 11 in the 1911 report).

"12. It creates positions (membership in the commission) which should be attractive to first-class citizens, since the service offers opportunities for high usefulness without interruption of their private careers.

"MINORITY REPORT

"By Ernest S. Bradford.

"Greater unity in city government, which is coming to be demanded in some commission-governed cities, can best be secured by giving the mayor more power than the other commissioners, thus placing him in the position to properly coördinate the activities of all departments and to compel, if necessary, unity of action. This is in line with previous recommendations of the National Municipal League, which has favored a strong mayor. It is doubtful whether the idea should be carried as far as it is applied in Houston, Texas, but it may be desirable to experiment in this direction. The mayor would, in this case, become the managing and directing force of the city.

"The city manager plan departs in several respects from commission government lines, and it is doubtful whether it should be classed as a mere variation of commission government rather than a brand new plan. It contemplates, we are told, the election of a commission unpaid, or receiving only nominal salaries. Most commissioners are paid, under the commission form, some well paid; many devote their entire time to city affairs.

"The city manager plan permits election by wards. Every commission-governed city so far has abandoned ward elections.

"The city manager plan should be tried and the results secured under its operation impartially examined; but it should not be classed under the head of the commission form until it is very clear that it substantially agrees with the important features of that form. The same credentials should be required of this new plan as were held necessary in the case of the commission form, i. e., evidence that under it municipal conditions are better than they were under the aldermanic form; and in addition, the evidence should be clear that the city manager plan is superior to the commission form, before the latter, now tested for ten years and more, is relinquished for a new and untried type of government."

A thought-provoking statement is that of Hon. William Dudley Foulke, who said, in addressing the Toronto meeting of the National Municipal League:

"It seems to me this entire question of the preference of one system over the other is a question of the adaptability of the particular form to the habits, to the prejudices and to the political status of the different cities to which they are to be applied. I take it that in the end the municipal manager system will be found the one best adapted to cities in a general way. But when it comes to applying it now to cities which have been accustomed to political methods, and are still subject to boss rule, I am inclined to believe it might be very injurious.

"This is a kind of reform we should not hurry too much; we ought to await developments, and I am very glad that the city manager plan has been preceded by the commission form of government, and that over three hundred cities have already adopted that form. This will do a great work in eliminating the boss systems by which our municipalities in the United States have so largely been controlled. It will thereby lead public opinion to regard city governments more and more as largely business affairs and to be administered if not entirely upon business principles, at least upon principles of common decency and morality. After they have reached that state and after politics in its worst form has become eliminated, is the time for the city manager system to be applied.

"For the present, however, if you apply that system, I can see what the result will often be, that it may not be an improvement on the commission plan, but will be even worse than the old plan by which we have been governed. I think I can see the man who has been our mayor for a great many years, although we now have got him out. I think we know exactly how Doc Zimmerman would act if the city manager plan were now put on in the city of Richmond. He would lay his plans for the place before the election—the place, not of mayor, but of city manager, and he would have his slate of five commissioners who would go in and vote for him, and he would get men who were personally popular and knew how to pull the ropes. His skill as a politician is much better than that of the men who would oppose him. He would have his five men who would vote for him, and the issue before election would be, 'Are we to have Doc Zimmerman for manager or not?'

"It is far better to vote for a man directly instead of indirectly, as we have done in the election of United States senators and in the election of the President of the United States. When the Constitution was adopted it was considered that the best way to elect a president was not to have the whole body of people vote, but to have a selected body or college who would meet and find out by some means—by the inspiration of the spirit or something—who was the best man to become President of the United States; the people could not be trusted to do that work. It was the same way in electing senators—not to trust the whole body of the people, but to have the Legislature think the thing over and choose the man they wanted. But the people of the United States have now determined by constitutional amendment that it is better for the people to choose by direct election than by this indirect method which confuses and obscures the issues and often degrades the electoral bodies and makes mere dummies out of the men who compose them. That would be the result in cities still subject to the political usages which now prevail in many parts of the country. Therefore, it would be a very bad thing for the National Municipal League to recommend the immediate adoption of a system like that to places that are not ready for it.

"Let all cities that are ripe for business administration, all cities that have abolished political ideas in their city government—let them take the city manager plan. But for those which have not, which do not yet know how to get rid of the bosses, I think it would be a dangerous experiment.

"Suppose instead of calling him the city manager, you call him the city boss; you can see how the plan would work out in a community habituated not to a manager, but to a boss. So let us go slow.

"'How many things by season seasoned are
To their right praise and true perfection!'

"There is a doubt as to whether the manager system has yet been tried far enough for us to express a definite opinion as to whether it is yet preferable everywhere to the other system, though I believe this will ultimately be the case."

In an article read before the Ohio League of Municipalities in January, 1914, at Columbus, Ohio, Commission Manager Charles E. Ashburner, of Springfield, Ohio, said substantially as follows:

"There are some advocates of the commission form where the commissioners divide the work, each taking the management of some department.

If there is success in that form of government in small cities, I think it can only be a matter of luck. How can voters select men, three or four, who have knowledge of the branches of government they are supposed to manage? Again the salaries necessary to pay three or four competent men are prohibitory in a small city. No man can successfully manage any branch of municipal affairs unless he devote his entire time, thought and energies to the particular work and if he does this he will become absorbed in his particular branch and be unable to do justice to other branches when he meets with the other commissioners on the general business of the city. Imagine three perfect departmental heads, all of whom are commissioners, meeting and trying to be unbiased in the division of the tax duplicate. Show me a good department head, I will show you a bad commissioner. The only possible connecting link between the legislative and the operative branches is the hired manager. The commissioner is the director—he is the same man you find in the Standard Oil Company, the railroad, the bank, the local ice company or in any other corporation. He is the keen business man who does not pretend to interfere with the operating machinery but who knows when the man at the helm (the manager) is delivering the goods.

"It has been argued that men suitable for managers of cities are hard to find. True; because there has been small demand for such an article, but I am sure that they will develop as rapidly as the demand—so this is merely a ghost trouble. The real trouble with the business management of small cities is the fact that in small communities each citizen knows more about his neighbor's business than he does himself and such familiarity makes men cowardly when it comes to doing their duty, if such duty should offend their neighbor. The hired manager's future in life is dependent upon his fearless discharge of his duties. He may be turned down and crushed temporarily but the business men of this country are looking for such men. Another argument in favor of the hired employee—I hope I have not wearied you with my arguments for my manager form—I believe it is right, and having convinced myself, at least, I will try and show you the working plan of organization. First the commissioners, three or five, with nominal salary as a board of directors, one of whom (selected by the commission, to be president of the body) and for all legal purposes to occupy the position of mayor. The commission to hire a manager who shall hold office during the pleasure of the commission.

"The treasurer and auditor and solicitor should also be appointed by the commission, but every other city employee should be appointed by the city manager, who should, of course, be broad enough to allow the heads of departments to select their help. The manager armed with this authority should be held to strict account for results and should be removed whenever the commission find that they can improve the service by his absence.

"Nothing but strict, impartial, unbiased, honest, and fearless business should be tolerated in any city hall.

"America can and does produce the type of man necessary and as soon as a public conscience is aroused that will support such men, they will come out of the service of the big corporations and give their time to the citizens of our municipalities. Heretofore few clean men have been willing to accept the mud and slime of politics thrown upon those who dare to do their duty."

For this particular work, Mr. Ashburner has set forth his views upon the commission manager question thus:

"Believing as I do that the commission manager form of government comes nearer solving the problems of municipal administration than any other form heretofore in existence I would like to be recorded as one of those who does not believe, however, that the failure of the council form of government is due to the men who constitute, in a majority of cases, the councils of our cities.

"The average councilman in an American city is a self-sacrificing, honest citizen whose energies are expended in conducting a law office, a grocery, a drug-store or some other kind of work in order that he may provide a suitable living for himself and family, and yet, during a few hours each month, he attempts to act as a director in a municipal corporation handling affairs involving large sums of money, often allowing his vote to be influenced by those who have made it their business to see that some pet scheme is presented to him during his busy hours in its most favorable light. He is also handicapped by having each department a separate unit which does not coöperate with other units composing the city government and often he does not know what is the proper thing to do.

"It took some years for the American people to learn that this unqualified board of directors, notwithstanding their honesty, was a failure in giving to cities an economical and efficient administration. The next move was the commission form of government in which a various number of commissioners were elected by the people, these commissioners then constituting themselves into heads of various departments. This again is a weakness in that the voters cannot possibly elect three or five men who are experts in the various lines of work they take up as managing directors after their election. Suppose, also, that the five commissioners should be men capable of managing the various departments of the city government, is it not to be presumed that the expense of paying such men would be enormous? Allowing that the salaries justify the employment of high-class commissioners and allowing that chance has given to the people a man fitted for each position, we still have that weakness in human nature, namely, that no man can successfully manage any branch of municipal affairs unless he devote his entire time, thought and energies to his particular work and should he do this he will become absorbed in his particular branch and be unable to do justice to the other branches of the government when he meets with the other commissioners on the general business of the city.

"Success has come to the American business corporation through the organization of a board of directors who are capable business men and who are able to grasp a situation when presented to them in its various phases by an employee designated as the manager. Why should not success come to the municipal corporation from the same organization that has made the success of American business a by-word the world over?

"The manager should be a man with versatile qualifications, one who is not afraid to do what he believes right, and above all, one who will be absolutely frank and honest in his dealings with his board of directors.

"The fact that in six years, from a small beginning, the commission manager form is now in operation in sixteen different municipalities in this country, and that in no case have we heard of any desire to change back to any of the more ancient forms of administration speaks well for what, to my mind, is the most original, the most simple, and the most concentrated form of municipal organization."

Mr. Waite has expressed his views and some of his experiences in the succeeding article written for this book.

"THE CITY MANAGER FORM OF GOVERNMENT IN THE LIGHT OF EXPERIENCE

"There are two pertinent questions: first, 'Can the commission manager form of government be made successful?'—second, 'Can the commission manager form of government be made permanent, if successful?'

"Immediately after the Home Rule Amendment was passed in Ohio the thinking men of Dayton worked out a plan of action. The new charter was the result of their efforts.

"This charter comprises the basic form of organization used in all large corporations. Mr. Patterson, president of the National Cash Register Company, the ruling spirit, used the rule of five which he uses in all of his own organization charts —five commissioners elected at large and non-partisan, and five departments. The flood of Dayton aided in bringing the people together. Party lines were obliterated. Five sound business men were elected as commissioners. They selected the manager. The manager selected the directors of the five departments.

"The director of law was on the charter commission as its legal representative. The director of finance was a public accountant. The director of welfare was a minister, broad, intelligent, doing his greatest work outside of his church. The director of service is an engineer trained in municipal work, and brought to Dayton for this service. The director of safety has not been appointed; the manager is acting director. All the men selected are trained for the particular functions which they direct. I cannot tell you the political faith of the commissioners or of the directors. They were selected for their ability. There were no political debts to be paid. Our energies have been expended on progressive and constructive lines. We have not attempted the sensational.

"Careful, expert investigations have preceded all new plans.

"Expert engineers have worked out intelligent plans for improvements in the waterworks, looking well into future requirements. Expert engineers have investigated and made report on the proper distribution of city wastes. Expert engineers are advising us in the plans for the development of a comprehensive sewer system.

"In a similar way, we have investigated crime and social conditions, police and fire departments, parks and playgrounds, city planning, and grade elimination.

"In our finance department, our new accounting system is the same as would be found in any large business. Our budget is scientific. Every month the head of each department receives a complete financial statement which shows the original allowance, expenditures and balance in each account. We keep our expenditures inside our allowances.

"In August we found that our estimated revenues were too high. With our system of accounting and budget, we were enabled, in two days, to reduce expenditures forty-five thousand dollars, and reorganize all work accordingly. It was customary to issue bonds for current expenses. This practice has been stopped. We inherited a promissory note the first of the year for one hundred and twenty-five thousand dollars in the safety department, which was paid in February. This will be reduced this year over twenty-five thousand dollars. All current funds in the treasury have been put into one. It has not been necessary to borrow any additional money on this note up to this time, and we will save five thousand dollars in interest.

"Our purchasing department will save twenty thousand dollars this year. Every department has unit cost systems. Efficiency is maintained by the deadly parallel.

"Police and fire drills have been enforced. Civil service records show merits and demerits. The men are listed on the results of examinations as well as by daily performances. Policewomen are aiding in the handling of women derelicts and domestic troubles.

"The organization is keyed up to preventive methods.

"The fire department is continually making house to house inspections, reducing fire hazard. Workhouse prisoners are used on municipal improvements, parks, cleaning and repairing streets. A municipal lodging house has been established. The inmates are worked one-half day. All philanthropic and city nursing has been combined into the welfare department, thus saving all duplication of effort. District surgeons have been appointed; three baby clinics and milk stations have been established.

"In the months of June, July, August, September and October, the death rate of babies of under one year has been reduced forty per cent. over last year. One general, and two tuberculosis, clinics have been established.

"School children have been joined in a Civic Workers' League and help to keep the city clean. Prizes have just been awarded to the school districts showing the greatest improvement. Children's and back yard gardens have been awarded prizes. Any family or neighborhood willing to clean up empty lots, was aided by the city removing the rubbish, and plowing the lots. Four hundred lots were cleaned and plowed; four hundred dirty spots were turned into four hundred gardens which furnished vegetables to four hundred families, and gave a new interest to them.

"The Civic Music League has been established; concerts have been given in community centers and choruses organized. A series of six concerts to be given by foremost artists and symphonies, has been arranged for the winter of 1914-15, at a rate of three dollars and a half for the season. Twenty-five hundred seats, which is the capacity of the hall, have been sold.

"In ten months much has been accomplished, and economically accomplished. The city manager form of government can be made successful.

"As to the second question in your mind, 'Can this success be made permanent?'—the answer to this question lies with the people.

"The American people are habituated to the idea of change. It is customary when we have elected one party into power, to have the other party or parties immediately start a campaign to show us why that party should be out of power. We are restless for change. It is inbred in the nation. The results accomplished by the new form of government now coming into use, can as yet, scarcely be grasped by the very people who have voted these governments into power.

"Each new improvement offends someone's prejudices or purse. Too many new improvements breed too many centers of discontent. As a people we are fickle; we learn by experience and slowly, and often through waste. These new forms of municipal government have many ups and downs ahead of them. We love to live as we have lived. Changes with which we are not in complete sympathy we are prone to define as whims. Every citizen is an expert on all municipal questions. Our duty, your duty, is to educate the people to appreciate the possibilities of these new forms of government which we have called into being. There, to my mind, now lies the greatest work. Publicity must be given to the results obtained by the new governments. We must obtain an efficient citizenship. Interest should be maintained through the schools. We need fewer elections, longer terms, and thereby greater efficiency.

"The commission manager form of government can be made a success. . . . Its permanency depends upon an intelligent citizenship, and their continued determination to keep partisan politics out of municipal affairs."

Dayton Charter Faults.—Professor Herman G. James has set forth succinctly the vital objections opponents of the city manager plan find in it. He is specifically objecting to the Dayton charter, and says:

"The first of these weaknesses is found at the very beginning of the charter where in section 1 an enumeration of the powers of the corporation is attempted. Now it is a well-recognized fact that the practice of enumerating the corporate powers of cities has been the source of great inconvenience, in this country. No enumeration can ever be complete and so it is necessary to add, as has been done in section 2 of the Dayton charter, that 'enumeration of particular powers by this charter shall not be held or deemed to be exclusive, but, in addition to the powers enumerated herein, implied thereby or appropriate to the exercise thereof, the city shall have, and may exercise all other powers which under the constitution and laws of Ohio it would be competent for this charter specifically to enumerate.' Even if such a blanket provision effected its purpose, namely, to confer upon the city all local powers so far as possible under the laws and constitution, we would at least have to conclude that the enumeration in section 1 is surplus verbiage. But that is not all, for courts have repeatedly taken the view that the principle of *inclusio unius, exclusio alterius* will be applied whenever there is an enumeration of such corporate powers, and that a blanket clause like that of section 2 above will not be given effect. Hence such an enumeration so far from being of any benefit may be a positive detriment. Much better, therefore, would it be, to make a general grant of powers subject to the limitations imposed in the charter.

"The second feature of the Dayton charter which it would seem undesirable for other cities to copy relates to the nomination provision. More than two pages are taken up with regulations concerning primary elections, when it would have been much simpler to provide for nomination by mere declaration, on the English plan. Primary elections are no doubt superior to the old packed convention system of party nomination, but where it is the avowed purpose of a charter, as it is that of the Dayton charter to have 'party politics eliminated' it is unnecessary to have any kind of formal nomination procedure. Primary elections double the cost of elections, and, what is worse, they double the burden of the elector, which means just that much less participation by the voters, especially the best fitted ones. If a multiplicity of candidates is feared, it is suggested that the probability of minority candidates being chosen as a result of many applicants is on the one hand not a real danger and on the other can be met in a simple manner. That facility in becoming a candidate does not necessarily lead to a plethora of aspirants is shown by the experience of England. But even if it should do so in this country the danger of minority choices can be met by the use of the preferential ballot.

"The third objectionable feature of the Dayton charter is of much greater significance because it seems to strike right at the heart of the city manager principle. By section 13 of the charter *the city manager is made subject to recall.* Now it seems clear that the very first step in the direction of expert city administration was to take the choice of the experts out of the hands of the electorate and to put it into the hands of some other organ, the council or the mayor as the case might be. It was felt that this offered greater opportunity of getting an expert man in the first place and of having him administer the affairs of the city energetically, without continually weighing in his mind the probable effects of enforcing this or that administrative measure which might be disagreeable to this or that influential political individual or group. If it is characteristic of the city manager plan to make the commission or council responsible for choosing the best man for the place, what possible justification can there be for making that same man subject to recall by the electorate? If he must 'make a hit with the people' to keep from being recalled, he is scarcely in a better situation than if he has to make a hit with the people to be elected in the first place and his motives will inevitably be influenced by the contemplation of what response this or that proposed improvement will meet with in the minds of the voter."

Counter-arguments.—A counter-argument to his first objection is that all the rights of the city are secured by the phrase he objects to, however verbose; and those versed in law and who must contend with its technicalities learn that words and seemingly needless provisions in the eyes of the layman may take on vital significance when tested by the local rules of law according to which they must stand or fall; this charter of Dayton was drawn under the supervision of able lawyers familiar with specific statutes of the General Code of Ohio. Advocates of the Dayton charter will urge that the objection, therefore, shall not be given too much weight. However, the plan itself is not vitally affected one way or the other.

The second objection depends for its weight upon local conditions. The Socialists in some communities prefer the preferential ballot and other factions or other communities prefer other forms. No one form is essential to the city manager idea. The people of Ohio and, in this particular instance, Dayton, were thoroughly conversant with the primary elections; and knowing how to handle and achieve very excellent results, it was very wise to retain that feature when so many innovations were being introduced already.

In regard to the third objection, those who cannot agree with it say that there is no difference between recalling a commission because the manager is unsuitable and recalling the manager direct. In fact, they claim the latter is more in keeping with the direct government idea of the city manager plan in that the executive proving unsuitable, they remove him, without disturbing the legislative commission with whose policies they may be in entire sympathy and whom they may wish to retain, while they do not care to keep the manager whom the commission selected, and whose methods of execution are displeasing. It is also easier to remove one man than attack a number of the commission; the removal of the manager might alone be sufficient to insure popular desires being complied with without removal of the commission, because of its salutary effect. Nevertheless, removal of both manager and commission by recall is provided for.

CHAPTER XIV

ADVANTAGES AND DISADVANTAGES

Officials in commission cities do not need the boss because he can give them nothing.

BRUÈRE

ARGUMENTS FOR OLD FORM

In behalf of the conventional form of city administration, its advocates have advanced certain stock arguments. Those who so earnestly desire the retention of that system have argued that decentralization of power in the new government will be the chiefest evil. They claimed, and it is a fine sounding phrase in a political speech, that democracy should not tolerate the exercise of a great amount of power by any one man. Let no one official, greedy of power, control a major part of the government! We agree. Yet, practically, it has been found that where a small amount of power is given each official, this fragmentary authority when abused was too small to locate or too minute to justify a large expenditure to correct; that responsibility was shifted from one official to another with the remark that he was not responsible, but that a certain other official was, while the next official claimed still another was chargeable in the premises; and so on in an exasperating meandering through the labyrinth of public office. That was the practical result of decentralization of power and responsibility, and one radically different from the happy view of it in campaign literature.

Responsibility to Popular Will.—The old form was a more flexible government, pliant to the will of the people, it was claimed, because each officer was responsible to his constituents. But who were his constituents? That was the crucial, if somewhat embarrassing, question. Experience proved that an official was put into power by a political leader under cover of party principles and practices, and naturally the official in a very human way customarily regarded the party, using the short term for the party leader, as his constituents. It was quite true an official felt responsible to his constituents, but the people a major part of the time experienced little of this adherence to their own interests. The maxim that public service is a public duty has not always been the motto in city halls.

Wards.—The same adverse criticism applies to the ward system. The sentimental idea that a man, elected from a section of the city, would be in active touch and sympathy with its particular needs, was calculated to touch the heart strings of the voters. It was a fine sentiment and excellent politics; but in actual practice displayed a distressing result. It has been found in this arrangement of the old city that an alderman harkened to the political boss in his ward, rather than to its public needs; that it was a scheme for trading political "sugar plums," rather than a position the occupant of which displayed an intuitive faculty in divining the needs of his fellow-townsmen.

Separation of Powers.—Furthermore, these proponents of the traditional municipal government advanced the claim that legislative and executive functions must be separate. So they should. Nevertheless, the application of the principle in the former governments was so erroneous as to fail in achieving adequate results. The executive power under the old mayor and council plan coupled with a veto, gave the mayor a control unwarranted and unnecessary in municipal affairs. A veto in state or national government is a very beneficial prerogative, but the city presents another problem, when considered in comparison with projects of purely political significance. The usual council was unwieldy; was frequently dominated by political interests; was incoherent in organization because of the transaction of business by ill-organized committees, whose proceedings were often secret in character or ill-recorded. This body has been justly arraigned on charges of irresponsiveness to public will, extravagance, incompetence, political favoritism and legislative action founded on whim rather than on exact knowledge. To retain the legislative idea, but abolish the signal shortcomings, was the aim of the charter framers. How justified they were in their efforts, the records of deficits, gross incompetence, and criminal extravagance are mute witnesses.

Minorities.—Thus stood the main arguments for the conventional city government. Its survival for several hundred years is of no other significance than that it has had a fair trial. Its present faults and inadequacies should decree its exit. As the reasons why local and national politics should be alienated have already been discussed, there remains only the question as to whether the new government will mean the abolition of parties and strong minorities. Parties may be depended upon so long as human views differ. It is true that the old system of minorities will disappear, but only in kind, not in substance. The minority in a political machine has been so often subsidiary to the dominant party, or conspicuous principally because so ineffective; its departure will be only notable because of the passing of the fine art in political graft. Parties are essential, but in local government they must be built on different issues and different lines from present city politics.

Essentials.—Three radical principles are essential to a modern municipal administration. First, candidates must be tested on the basis of efficiency, not political faithfulness; technical men must be selected for technical jobs and business men for policy-forming positions. Second, publicity and responsibility of a few well-known men are the necessary prerequisites for results. Third, business methods must be utilized in a business corporation.

ARGUMENTS FOR CITY MANAGER PLAN

These three vital objects were the ambition of the charter framers of the city manager plans. Efficiency, publicity, and concentrated responsibility stand the triple commandments of the new gospel of government.

Efficiency.—Business of any complication demands trained men to guide it. Municipal officers are no exception to the rule. England, Germany and France have a body of municipal officials of long training who regard the work as a professional man would regard his own. Why should not we, being of practical genius, adopt so obvious a plan? We are adopting one. We have not done so sooner, for one excellent reason, because there has been until now no class of men of this type from which to draw competent municipal executives.

We have a professional administrator now. The city manager plan secures efficiency through the employment of an expert municipal governor. His technical training, his business experience, and his knowledge of city needs are valuable adjuncts to executive ability. They are the highroad for the application of his personality. This insures efficiency.

Concentration.—The civic system is simplified. The whole city is unified under one management; the municipality is vigorously controlled under one competent responsible head. A city, no more than an individual, can realize its fullest promise under a dual personality. The city manager plan provides, therefore, concentrated responsibility.

The legislative function is left unimpaired. Men of sound business experience under this plan can feel free to accept, without detriment to their private interests, the position of commissioner. It is

ADVANTAGES AND DISADVANTAGES 261

within the scope of their experience and they can bring to the position the valuable ideas of a ripe business judgment; and furthermore, this plan contemplates that this body of business men, styled the commission, who are trained in the selecting and fitting of men to their duties, shall select the manager. The selection of the chiefest personal factor is left to them. Two advantages result. On the one hand, there is no trust put in the dangerous method of allowing a selection of an expert by popular elections at short intervals; on the other hand, the people do not have the restriction imposed on them in selecting commissioners, of electing at the same time in the same persons those who are capable of the twin duties of legislation and administration.

Publicity.—Intelligent action of a voter can only be exercised when he is thoroughly equipped with reliable information. Public hearings on the budget, readable and understandable publications as to the city's financial and physical condition, a public reason publicly stated for the transaction of a public affair, all constitute a great guardianship of civic interests. To know is to understand, to understand is to interest, to interest is to treat with success.

The Dayton Bureau of Municipal Research published the following excellent summary of the advantages of the city manager plan:

"1. There is the same concentration of power and responsibility found in the regular commission plan.

"2. The elections are non-political and for long terms of office.

"3. The interests of the citizens are safeguarded by initiative, referendum and recall.

"4. The plan has the added advantage of separating legislative from executive duties.

"5. Employment of trained administrators for long terms is assured.

"6. Should an appointive officer fail to make good, he can be removed instantly.

"7. The plan is similar to the organization of business enterprises, and continental cities where its success has been amply proven.

"8. The extension of the Civil Service and independence of the Board of Elections will absolutely prevent the building of a political machine by either the Manager or the Commissioners."

ARGUMENTS AGAINST THE CITY MANAGER PLAN

Good men can be found in any city to run it, is the traditional maxim of local politics. Such is

ADVANTAGES AND DISADVANTAGES 263

the argument in opposition to the new plan. And this may be quite true so far as ability is concerned. There is inevitably a radical advantage in having a man of ability coupled with a mind fresh to a new situation, keen to grasp the original problems, and open to persuasion, unshackled as he is by the fetters of tradition and old ideals. No clique or party or political organization or reform movement would have any predominant claim upon him. Long-continued influence of an environment will inevitably have a profound hold on any man, and this provision affords opportunity to avoid the evil consequences of it.

It must be understood, nevertheless, that the selection of a man outside of the city is permissible and not necessary; the provision is for the sake of the securing the best without handicap. Opponents of the plan claim that it is too novel and adventurous an idea, foreign in character and unadaptable to American conditions, and therefore a plan of failure and disaster and ominous consequences. Again, the elections at large will be the means of slighting special localities and favoring others unduly, while the old method of having a section or ward represented by a special resident of that district insured protection for his ward and equal share in all good things. The history of the ward system presents to this proposition an embarrassing counter-argument; the long years of corruption and "log-rolling" for special favors by each councilman, and the disheartening lack of results would even justify a more desperate defense than this salutary remedy of general elections. It is suggested that the salaries are too high and that talent sufficient for the duties can be had at much lower rates. If time proves that economy is effected by employing high-salaried men, and it will not take a great while to determine it, then this argument will be relegated to the company of its predecessors. So run arguments and counter arguments.

The special advantages of the Springfield (Ohio) charter are set forth by their charter commission as follows:

1. It secures Home Rule for Springfield.

2. It establishes a simple, direct and businesslike form of government.

3. It makes elective officers responsive to public opinion by means of the initiative and referendum.

4. It provides for direct primaries and a non-partisan ballot.

5. It prohibits candidates from soliciting office by improper methods.

6. It affords to capable men the opportunity of

holding office during good behavior, thus tending to the development of trained public servants.

7. It furnishes, through the recall, a simple method of removing inefficient or corrupt officials.

8. It requires public hearings upon money appropriations.

9. It secures full publicity of official acts, yet eliminates wasteful methods of legal advertising.

10. It creates a purchasing department which will effect great saving in the purchase of supplies.

11. It permits public work to be done by direct labor as well as by contract.

12. It fixes eight hours as a day's labor upon public work.

13. It safeguards the city in franchise matters.

14. It offers a means of avoiding much unnecessary tearing up of streets for service connections.

15. It recognizes the people as the sole source of governmental power and imposes upon each member of the community the duty and responsibility of actively interesting himself in the affairs of the city.

The Research Bureau claims the hereinafter enumerated advantages for the Dayton (Ohio) charter:

1. A continuous audit of city accounts, with a

general balance sheet exhibiting assets and liabilities of the city.

2. The requirement of summaries of city income and expenditure rather than of receipts and expense.

3. Accounting procedure adequate to record in detail all transactions affecting the acquisition, custodianship and disposition of values.

4. A scientific budget classified uniformly for the main functional divisions of all departments.

5. Standardization and centralized purchasing of all supplies.

6. Time sheets and certification of all payrolls.

7. Current financial and operating statements exhibiting each transaction and the cost thereof.

8. Adequate franchise control.

9. Citizen-boards to consult and advise with the various departments.

10. Standardization of service and compensation, insuring equal pay for equal work in every branch of the city government.

CONCLUSION

The foregoing arguments pro and con are presented as they appeared in the campaigns for the new municipal organizations. They are the development of much political struggle, a wide movement of reform, a deep-seated sense of unrest. Their value rides on their face and they are designed to appeal to the same class who read this chapter— the voters.

APPENDIX A

CITY GOVERNMENT BY COMMISSION

A REPORT OF THE NATIONAL MUNICIPAL LEAGUE

The committee finds itself in agreement on the following interpretations of features of commission government:

MAJOR FEATURES

1. *Commission government is a relative success* as compared with the older forms. The people who live under it are generally more content. They feel that they are more effective politically and that commission government is an asset to their town. Substantial financial improvements have generally resulted, demonstrating a striking increase in efficiency and a higher standard of municipal accomplishment, and this may fairly be credited to the better working of the new plan.

2. This relative success of commission government

results *primarily because it is more democratic* (i. e., sensitive to public opinion) than the old form. Among the features which undoubtedly are responsible for this increased sensitiveness are

a. *Its "unification of powers,"* as contrasted with the old undesirable "separation of powers." The commission, having all the power, has no one to blame for failure to please the public, cannot evade full responsibility, and, having ample power to remedy each abuse, can be held responsible for any failure to do so. This stripping away of the old-time protective confusion of responsibility exposes the commission to the direct fire of public opinion and makes its members personally targets for public criticism. The unification of powers unifies the whole governmental system, gives the government the single controlling brain which is necessary to a successful organism, prevents lost motion, "pulling and hauling," deadlocks, and ill feeling.

b. *The short ballot.* This makes each elective official conspicuous on election day and after; makes intelligent voting so easy that practically every citizen can vote intelligently without any more conscious effort than he expended on his business of citizenship under the old plan. The short ballot simplifies the whole work of citizenship so much that the citizens can handle their political affairs without employing a political machine as an intermediary political instrument. The short ballot in small cities makes the politician and his machine superfluous, and thereby substitutes for the old oligarchy of political experts a democracy in which the entire populace participate.

Being acutely sensitive and therefore anxious to please, commission government has been giving the people better government because the people are and always have been ready to applaud honest and progressive government. A contributing factor undoubtedly is the fact that the radical change has usually awakened a fresh civic interest among the citizens, which runs along of its own momentum for a considerable time and does much to tone up every branch of administration.

Commission government could reasonably be expected to succeed with these features (unification of powers and the short ballot) alone, and no new city charter should ever be classified as true commission government which lacks these essentials.

Other Features

3. *Non-partisan ballot.* The non-partisan method of election is highly desirable, but not absolutely indispensable, as the short ballot, by making the party label a superfluous convenience, thereby destroys much of the label's influence, anyway.

4. *The initiative and referendum-by-protest* have proved useful as provisions for allaying the time-honored, popular fear of intrusting large powers to single bodies. The sensitiveness of commission government reduces the necessity for these devices and instances of their use in commission governed cities are very uncommon. It should not be forgotten that Galveston and Houston, the first two cities to have the plan, made their success without these features. They have not proved dangerous or susceptible to misuse.

5. *The recall* is a desirable, but not indispensable extension and modification of the right to elect. We have no evidence that it has been misused. In several cases it seems to have been employed to good advantage. Under the sensitive commission plan it is less needed than with the old plan, and is more practical.

6. *The abolition of ward lines* is desirable in small cities, and has been generally welcomed as putting an

end to numerous petty abuses. It tends to prevent petty log-rolling and emphasizes the unity of the city. Its importance, however, has been generally overestimated, for there are many cities (Galveston, before the flood, being one) where ward lines have been abolished without developing any appreciable or permanent reform.

7. It is unsound, and therefore unwise, to make the commission *auditor* of its own accounts. This does not necessarily involve the independent election of a city auditor in all cities. Some authority, such as the Governor, could appoint a state officer with power to investigate the accounts of all cities and to make his reports public. This is in line with the National Municipal League's familiar demand for uniform municipal accounting and reporting.

8. It is unsound to give the commission control over the *civil service commission,* as in Des Moines, unless the civil service commission be given a protected and long tenure of office and rotation of appointment. The civil service commission might better be appointed by some remote authority, such as the Governor.

9. *Mayor's veto. It is doubtful whether the mayor should have a veto* over his *confrères,* or, in fact, any added powers, lest he overshadow the other commis-

sioners and attract the limelight at their expense, leaving them in obscurity, where the people cannot intelligently and justly criticize and control them.

Applicability to Different Sized Cities

10. Commission government is in general to be recommended for cities of 100,000 population and under, and possibly also for cities of much larger size, in preference to any other plan now in operation in any American city.

The maximum size which may wisely adopt the commission plan without any modification cannot as yet be established, as too few large cities have tried it.

The foregoing represents matters on which the whole committee substantially agree.

The following are questions on which the committee did not agree and as practically all our work was done by correspondence it was impossible for the members to reason with each other and reach a conclusion. These matters are therefore submitted without conclusions in the form of subjects for further debate with a brief for each side.

11. *Should the election-at-large feature be retained in the case of very large cities?*

Yes. The abolition of the ward system in Boston brought excellent results in the composition of the council and is credited with having accomplished more in the way of breaking down the influence of the machine than any other feature of the new charter.

No. As the size of an electorate increases, the expense and difficulty of conducting campaigns for the office increases also, until they reach a scale where individual candidatures are balked and the support of an experienced political machine, as contrasted with that of a newly improvised machine, becomes so important to the success of a candidate as to give to existing machines a safe option in the choice of hopeful candidates. Officials when elected will thus be indebted to the machine, and the machines share with the people in the control over the government which ought to belong to the people alone. If machines are to be abolished as influences in municipal politics, their monopoly must be broken and free competition established, and this can only be done by creating conditions under which electioneering machinery, adequate for the task, can be improvised in case the established organizations are insufficiently deferential to public opinion. For large cities, therefore, the commission plan should be changed to something more like the

English or German plan of government by a ward-elected council of popular representatives, or possibly a plan of proportional representation could be worked that would be better yet. The requirement of residence in the district should be abolished.

12. *Should the size of the commission be radically enlarged in the case of very large cities?*

Yes. Five men are too few to represent the varied elements of a great population and will be too far from the people to be able to analyze public opinion by direct contact. The commission should therefore be enlarged but in a manner which will retain the short ballot. For moderate-sized cities, the choice of only a part of the commission at a time would help, but in the larger cities a subdivision of the people by ward divisions or proportional representation seems advisable.

That a large body is not fitted for executive work is admitted (though such government succeeds in British cities), but the executive function can be delegated to a compact appointive committee, or, better, to an appointive chief executive as in German cities and in the so-called "Lockport (N. Y.) Plan."

No. The existence of the initiative, referendum and recall would be sufficient to keep any city government in touch with popular opinion.

The business of city government is almost wholly executive. The commission should therefore be an executive body first and last.

The theory that for very large cities the commission should be enlarged is erroneous, since based on the belief that the greater the number of men the better the representation, which does not follow. The enlargement of the commission is incompatible with the short ballot, unnecessary beyond seven or nine members and preferably five or less, and tends toward the same confusion and irresponsibility so prevalent under the present council system.

13. *Should the individual commissioners each be executive heads of departments?*

Yes. This feature is incidental to the "unification of powers" and a method of combining legislative and administrative control in the same body. Under many charters the commission is the legislative body, and individually the members of the commission, being each the head of a department, constitute the administrative force. The commission is not a body of experts but a board of general managers whose oversight and general direction is required, but who are to hire the experts and technical men for the various positions needed. It is not essential that the commission should be a true reflection of the population; but it is important that they (the commission) act for the entire population and represent it in the sense of looking after the welfare of the whole city. An advisory board consisting of laboring men, reformers, business men, some women, and all the other elements of the population might be a desirable help to a city governing body in formulating its course of action; but the real work must be done by a few men and these should be the commission.

There is no more danger of intrusting the individual commissioner with the carrying out of the will of his confrères on the commission than of trusting the president of a corporation to carry out the will of the board of directors of which he is a voting member.

No. The feature of the usual plan which makes the elected officers administrative heads is unsound (except in the smallest cities where the communal work is of so simple a nature that it may safely be intrusted to any man of general common-sense). Where the city work is considerable and technical, the requirements that elective officers shall be competent to perform executive duties is a denial of accurate representation to many large classes of the community, for the requirements practically attempt to limit the people to the selection of members of the employer class. Experts and executives cannot be effectively selected by popular vote, and their choice is not a natural popular function. The interest of the people is in representation. The commission should be a true reflection of the population. In a city with a large laboring class, the commission should contain a due proportion of laboring men, and in the natural desire for such representation *the people will elect such men anyway* regardless of their unfitness by experience for large administrative work.

A list of commission-governed cities of over 25,000 population follows. There are, in addition, many more commission-governed towns of less than 25,000 population. The total population living under commission government June 1, 1914, is 7,705,735.

Commission-Governed Cities Over 25,000 Population

Alabama....... Birmingham, Mobile, Montgomery.
California...... Berkeley, Oakland, Pasadena, Sacramento, San Diego.
Colorado....... Colorado Springs, Denver.
Illinois........ Bloomington, Decatur, Elgin, Springfield.

APPENDIX A

Iowa..........Burlington, Cedar Rapids, Des Moines, Sioux City.
Kansas........Kansas City, Topeka, Wichita.
Kentucky......Covington, Lexington, Newport.
Louisiana......New Orleans, Shreveport.
Massachusetts..Haverhill, Lawrence, Lowell, Lynn, Salem, Taunton.
Michigan......Battle Creek, Saginaw.
Minnesota.....Duluth, St. Paul.
Missouri.......Joplin.
Nebraska......Lincoln, Omaha.
New Jersey....Atlantic City, Jersey City, Orange, Passaic, Trenton.
North Carolina. Wilmington.
Ohio..........Dayton, Springfield.
Oklahoma......Muskogee, Oklahoma City.
Oregon........Portland.
Pennsylvania...Allentown, Altoona, Chester, Easton, Erie, Harrisburg, Hazleton, Johnstown, McKeesport, New Castle, Reading, Wilkesbarre, Williamsport, York.
South Carolina. Columbia.
Tennessee......Chattanooga, Knoxville, Memphis, Nashville.
Texas.........Austin, Dallas, Fort Worth, Galveston, Houston, San Antonio.

Utah..........Ogden, Salt Lake City.
Washington....Spokane, Tacoma.
West Virginia..Huntington.
Wisconsin.....Oshkosh, Superior.

APPENDIX B

CITIES UNDER THE CITY MANAGER PLAN
JUNE 1, 1914

	Adopted	Population
Sumter, S. C.	6/12/12	8,109
Hickory, N. C.	4/—/13	3,716
Morganton, N. C.	4/—/13	2,712
Dayton, Ohio	8/12/13	116,577
Springfield, Ohio	8/26/13	46,921
La Grande, Ore.	10/1/13	4,843
Phœnix, Ariz.	10/10/13	11,134
Morris, Minn.	11/—/13	1,685
Amarillo, Texas	11/18/13	14,485
Terrell, Texas	11/—/13	7,050
Cadillac, Mich.	12/9/13	8,375
Manistee, Mich.	12/15/13	12,381
Montrose, Colo.	1/—/14	3,254
Abilene, Kans.		4,118

APPENDIX C

SOME ACID TESTS OF CITY MANAGER GOVERNMENT FROM THE FIRST NINETY DAYS OF OPERATION

(Dayton Bureau of Municipal Research)

Jan. 3.—Began the installation of an accounting system adequate to provide balance sheets of all city accounts, and provide exact control over public funds.

Jan 5.—Resolution limiting city expenditures to within actual revenues.

Jan. 8.—Provided for the purchasing of all city supplies by a central purchasing agent.

Jan. 13.—Engineering firm engaged to make survey of needs, and to recommend steps necessary to secure an adequate water supply. Blowing new wells and tying them into water supply.

Jan. 14.—Weekly school for policemen started, giving instruction in ordinances and character of duties; target practice and duels.

Jan. 16.—Civic workers' league formed to secure the coöperation of children in a city-wide cleanup.

Jan. 17.—Consulting engineers employed to investigate best means to dispose of garbage and refuse.

Jan. 18.—Commission appointed to organize summer baseball leagues among school boys.

Jan. 19.—Began periodic flushing of downtown streets.

Jan. 22.—Duties of a city complaint station extended to include complaints of every character.

Jan. 23.—Collection of ashes and rubbish resumed, after year of non-collection throughout the city.

Jan. 26.—Held first public hearing on the estimates of city expenditures.

Jan. 27.—Began fire prevention inspection of every residence and store building in Dayton.

Jan. 29.—Adequate clothing, shoes, socks, etc., supplied to prisoners in the workhouse.

Jan. 29.—Five district city physicians appointed for gratuitous service to those unable to pay.

Jan. 30.—Suggested and brought about the raising of funds by the women members of the Greater Dayton Association, for a survey of dependency, delinquency and kindred problems.

Feb. 1.—Secured thorough snow removal on downtown streets and directed police officers to require cleaning of sidewalks by householders.

Feb. 2.—Arranged to provide work for such needy cases as would be referred to the city by Associated Charities.

Feb. 6.—Commission named to draft a building code.

Feb. 10.—Municipal lodging house established.

Feb. 12.—Conference with railroad executives and agreement to minimize crossing blockades—street railway company reporting daily of crossing delays.

Feb. 15.—Street-car companies offer better ventilation of street-cars.

Feb. 16.—City commission passed first city budget to show salaries and costs in detail, and to group expenses according to uniform classification.

Feb. 17.—Conference with health officers of Miami Valley to promote efficient control of communicable diseases and clean milk supply.

Feb. 17.—Civic music league inaugurated. Choral societies being formed in the several parts of the city.

Feb. 20.—Commission appointed to revise and bring up to date the traffic ordinances of the city.

Feb. 21.—Free legal aid bureau formed to give advice to citizens unable to employ an attorney.

APPENDIX C

Feb. 24.—Seven additional patrolmen added to police force to patrol residence districts during the day.

Feb. 25.—Arranged for inauguration of "policewomen" service.

Feb. 26.—Unification of the visiting nurses of the city under the direction of the welfare department.

Mar. 1.—Upon request, street-car companies employ permanent switch tenders at central street intersections, to facilitate traffic movement.

Mar. 4.—Interested boy scouts in leading clean-up movement, organized play and garden development.

Mar. 6.—Work of the Playgrounds and Gardens Association united with the park and playground activities of the city.

Mar. 14.—Free baby clinic at office of the division of health established.

Mar. 16.—Free baby clinic established at Miami Valley and St. Elizabeth hospitals.

Mar. 18.—City secures vacant lots for those desiring gardens, and arrangements made for free plowing.

Mar. 20.—First bi-monthly meeting with dairymen held to promote safer milk supply.

Mar. 20.—Began rigid enforcement of traffic ordinance—"Safety first."

Mar. 26.—School of instruction for playground leaders opened.

Mar. 28.—Authorized the appointment of a Civic Plan Commission to pass on platting, and recommend plans for civic improvements.

Mar. 28.—Authorized the appointment of a commission on the renaming and renumbering of streets.

Mar. 30.—Began publicity on anti-fly and reduction of infant mortality campaign.

Mar. 30.—Adopted new uniforms and standards for the division of police.

Mar. 31.—Installed unit cost system on rubbish and ash removal, and garbage collection.

Mar. 31.—Began installation of unit cost system on livestock in division of fire.

Apr. 1.—Began installation of unit cost system in the municipal garage.

Apr. 4.—Installed unit cost system in city prison, municipal lodging house, and workhouse.

APPENDIX D

This was the form of pledge used to affiliate the Dayton voter with the charter movement:

PLEDGE CARD

I want a city government that provides the INITIATIVE, REFERENDUM, PROTEST and RECALL.

I want a commission of five citizens to legislate for Dayton under those restrictions.

I want the Commission to pick out for Dayton the best man that can be found as manager.

I want a Manager to be subject to recall and able to get one hundred cents' worth of service for every dollar expended.

I want the non-partisan ballot and a city government free from machine domination.

I PLEDGE myself to speak and work for the adoption of the COMMISSION-MANAGER PLAN of government in DAYTON.

Name........................
Address......................

And this is the way that voter was kept track of for the elections:

PRECINCT CARD

Name ....
Address ....
Politics ....
Is he for the new charter?....Yes......No......
Where employed.............................
Has he registered?.........................
   Report made by.........................
   Date..........Ward..........Prec..........

APPENDIX E

BIBLIOGRAPHY

Explanatory Comment.—The National Municipal League Report on "The Commission Plan and Commission-Manager Plan of Municipal Government" says of the sources of information on these subjects:

"The history of the movement is well described in Bradford's 'Commission Government in American Cities,' and Hamilton's 'Dethronement of the City Boss.' A symposium of the comments of various authoritative observers will be found in Woodruff's 'City Government by Commission.' Analyses of all the charters, together with the texts of the more significant ones, and other material suitable for the use of charter revision committees, will be found in Beard's 'Digest of Short-Ballot Charters,' a loose-leaf encyclopedia on the subject. The most thorough study of the administrative workings of commission government is Bruère's

'The New City Government,' comprising intensive examinations by representatives from the New York Bureau of Municipal Research. Literature for local campaigns for the adoption of the plan is obtainable from the National Short Ballot Organization in New York."

Activities of the Board of Public Welfare. Issued by Kansas City, Mo., Board of Public Welfare, 1913.

BAXTER, SYLVESTER. Berlin: A Study of Municipal Government in Germany. Salem Press Publishing and Printing Co., 1889.

BRADFORD, ERNEST S. Commission Government in American Cities. Macmillan, 1911.

BRUÈRE, HENRY. The New City Government. Appletons, 1912.

League of American Municipalities: Proceedings. Detroit, 1911.

MUNRO, W. B. The Government of European Cities. Macmillan, 1909.

Organization and Administration of the Department of Health of Dayton, Ohio. Dayton Bureau of Municipal Research, 1913.

SHAW, ALBERT. Municipal Government in England. Johns Hopkins University, 1888.

The Sumter "City Manager" Plan of Municipal

Government. Published by The Chamber of Commerce of Sumter, S. C., Feb., 1913.

Magazine Articles

AMERICAN CITY. "The Lockport Proposal: A City That Wants to Improve Commission Government." June, 1911.
"How a Little City Is Progressing Under a City Commissioner." July, 1913.
AMERICAN REVIEW OF REVIEWS. "Progress of the City Manager Plan." Feb., 1914.
ANNALS OF THE AMERICAN ACADEMY OF POLITICAL AND SOCIAL SCIENCE. "The Lockport Proposal," by F. D. Silvernail. Nov., 1911, xxxviii, No. 3.
ANNALS OF THE AMERICAN ACADEMY OF POLITICAL AND SOCIAL SCIENCE. May, 1912, xii.
ENGINEERING NEWS. "The City Manager Plan." May 13, 1913.
LITERARY DIGEST. "Dayton's Unique Charter." Aug. 30, 1913.
MUNICIPAL JOURNAL AND ENGINEER. "Dayton's New Government." Aug. 21, 1913.
"Springfield's New Government." Sept. 18, 1913.
NATIONAL MUNICIPAL REVIEW. "The Theory of

the New Controlled Executive Plan," by Richard S. Childs. Jan., 1913.

"The Vital Points in Charter Making from a Socialist Point of View," by Carl D. Thompson. July, 1913.

"The City Manager Plan," by L. D. Upson. Oct., 1913.

THE OUTLOOK. "The Practical Short Ballot." May 10, 1913.

"The City Manager Plan." Aug. 23, 1913.

THE PUBLIC. "The Municipal Business Manager." June 27, 1913.

THE SHORT BALLOT BULLETIN. The bi-monthly organ of the National Short Ballot Organization notes the progress of the City Manager plan in each issue.

WORLD'S WORK. "Progress of Simplified Municipal Government." June, 1913.

LIST OF REFERENCES ON THE CITY MANAGER PLAN FURNISHED BY COURTESY OF LIBRARY OF CONGRESS, DIVISION OF BIBLIOGRAPHY, DECEMBER 1ST, 1914

H. H. B. MAYER, *Chief Bibliographer*

1. American Academy of Political and Social Science, *Philadelphia*. Commission government and the city-manager plan; rev. ed. of

Commission government in American cities. Philadelphia, American academy of political and social science, 1914. 279 pp. (*Its* Annals.) H1. A4, v.

2. Beard, Charles A., ed. Digest of short ballot charters. A documentary history of the Commission form of municipal government. New York. Published by the Short Ballot organization (1911-   ), pp. 10001-91101.
"Definition of the 'City manager plan' ": pp. 10203-10204; City manager plan with proportional representation, by C. C. Hoag, pp. 21305-21310; City manager plan to date, by H. S. Gilbertson, pp. 21903-21906; Theory of the new controlled executive plan, by Richard S. Childs, pp. 21907-21910. JS342.B4.

3. Bureau of Municipal Research, *Dayton, O.* Shall we change our city government? A statement of three types of municipal government. (Federal plan—Commission plan —Commission-Manager plan.) Dayton, O., Bureau of municipal research (1913), 16 pp. JS805.3 1913.

4. Upson, Lent D. A charter primer. Dayton, O., Bureau of municipal research (1914), 24 pp. City Manager plan: pp. 8-11. JS805.3U7.

5. Woodruff, Clinton R., *ed*. City government by commission. New York, London, D. Appleton and company, 1911. 381 pp. (National municipal league series. v. 1.) JS342.W7.
   General manager for the city of Staunton, Va.: pp. 304-306.

Articles in Periodicals

6. 1913. Childs, Richard S. Theory of the new controlled-executive. National municipal review, Jan., 1913, v. 2: 76-81. JS39.N3, v. 2.
7. Hoag, C. G. The representative council plan of city government: The city manager plan improved by the applications of proportional representation to the election of the council. American city, Apr., 1913, v. 8: 373-380. HT101.A5, v. 8.
8. Gilbertson, H. S. Public administration: a new profession. American review of reviews, May, 1913, v. 47: 599-602. AP2.R4, v. 47.
9. Practical short ballot in Sumter. Outlook, May 10, 1913, v. 104: 50-51. AP2.O8, v. 104.
10. The growth of the city manager plan of municipal government. Engineering and contracting. May 21, 1913, v. 39: 565-566. TA201.E5, v. 39.

APPENDIX E

11. Progress of simpler municipal government. World's work, June, 1913, v. 26:236-237. AP2.W8, v. 26.
12. Embrey, A. T. How a little city is progressing under a city commissioner: Fredericksburg, Va. American city, July, 1913, v. 9: 25-27. HT101.A5, v. 9.
13. City manager plan. Outlook, Aug. 23, 1913, v. 104: 887-889. AP2.O8, v. 104.
14. Upson, L. D. The city manager plan of government for Dayton. National municipal review, Oct., 1913, v. 2: 639-644. JS39.N3, v. 2.
15. Dayton's step forward in city government. World's work, Oct., 1913, v. 26: 614. AP2.W8, v. 26.
16. Holden, A. M. Progress. American political science review, Nov., 1913, v. 7P: 653-655. JA1.A6, v. 7.
17. Riddle, Kenyon. The town manager as city engineer. American city, Dec., 1913, v. 9: 523-525. HT101.A5, v. 9.
18. Further comment on the possibilities of the city manager plan in municipal government. Engineering and contracting, Dec. 31, 1913, v. 40: 729. TA201.E5, v. 40.
19. Baker, Frederick. The commission plan vs. the

municipal business manager plan. Pacific municipalities, Dec., 1913, v. 27: 669-681. JS39.P3, v. 27.
20. Wilder, E. M. Commission and commission-manager forms contrasted. Pacific municipalities, Dec., 1913, v. 27: 689-693. JS39.P3, v. 27.
21. 1914. Bradford E. S., *and* H. S. Gilbertson. Commission form vs. city manager plan. American city, Jan., 1914, v. 10: 37-40. HT101.A4, v. 10.
22. City manager plan. American municipalities, Jan., 1914, v. 26: 113-114. JS39.C6, v. 26.
23. Marcosson, I. F. Business-managing a city. Collier's, Jan. 3, 1914, v. 52: 5-6. AP2.065, v. 52.
24. Driving politics out of Dayton. Literary digest, Jan. 24, 1913, v. 48: 147-148. AP2.L58, v. 48.
25. Coming of the city manager plan. National municipal review, Jan., 1914, v. 3: 44-48. JS39.N3, v. 3.
26. Gilbertson, H. S. Government and administration: The city manager plan. National municipal review, Jan., 1914, v. 3: 115-116. JS39.N3, v. 3.
27. James, H. G. Defects in the Dayton charter.

National Municipal charter. National municipal review, Jan., 1914, v. 3: 95-97. JS39.N3, v. 3.
28. The commission form of government. World's work, Jan., 1914, v. 27: 254-255. AP2.W8, v. 27.
29. Progress of the "City Manager" plan. American review of reviews, Feb., 1914, v. 49: 144-145. AP2.R4, v. 49.
30. Renwick, William W. Democracy chooses an autocrat. Technical world, Mar., 1914, v. 21: 13-19. T1.T2, v. 21.
31. Riddle, Kenyon. The manager plan of municipal government. Engineering news, Apr. 16, 1914, v. 71: 831-832. TA1.E6, v. 71.
32. City managers. (Dayton, O., Springfield, O.) Municipal world, Apr.. 1914, v. 24: 84. JS39.M78, v. 24.
33. Adopts City manager plan. American municipalities, May, 1914, v. 27: 51. (Montrose, Colo., pop. 3,254.) JS39.C6, v. 27.
34. Chase, Charles P. City manager plan for Iowa. American municipalities, May, 1914, v. 27: 58-60. JS39.C6, v. 27.
35. City manager plan successful in Clarinda, Ia. American municipalities, June, 1914, v. 27: 93. JS39.C6, v. 27.

36. Upson, L. D. How Dayton's city-manager plan is working. American review of reviews, June, 1914, v. 49: 714-717. AP2.R4, v. 49.
37. Waite, Henry M. "The city manager plan": how it operates in Dayton, O. Municipal journal, N. Y., June 4, 1914, v. 26: 822-823. TD1.M95, v. 26.
38. —— City manager plan—the application of business methods to municipal government. American city, July, 1914, v. 11: 11-13. HT101.A5, v. 11.
39. Kressly, Paul E. The city manager. Municipal engineering, July, 1914, v. 47: 15-18. JS39.C6, v. 47.
40. Childs, Richard S. Commission manager plan. Municipal Journal, N. Y., July 2, 1914, v. 37: 11.

INDEX

Accountant, city, 111
Accounting procedure, 112
Administrators, professional, 2; practical, 7
Alderman, 42
Amateurs v. professionals, 7
America, history repeats itself in, 31
American people, credit for idea due, 24
Ashburner, Chas. E., career of, 80; first city manager for Springfield, 80; first municipal experience of, in Staunton, 80; in Sumter, N. C., 81

Ballot, short, 6, 40; national short ballot organization, 170
Boards, civil service, 64; in Dayton, 66; rules of, 66; records of, 66; compensation of members of, 67; unclassified list of, 67; who compose, 67; compensation of, in Springfield, 68
Boards, miscellaneous, 64; consulting, 68; advisory, 69, 70; city plan, in Dayton, 71
Bond issues, table on, 12
Bruère, 255
Bryce, Rt. Hon. James, 36
Budget, scientific, 10; preliminary procedure in enactment of, 61; five fundamental objects of, 114; object of, in Dayton, 115; procedures, 123; procedures, vital elements of, 123.
Bürgermeister, duties of, 25; term of office of, 26; salary of, 26; powers and duties of, 27
Burke, Edmund, 155
Burton, Senator, 41
Business, private, and city government, 47

Charges, against administration, 6
Checks and balances, old system of, 37
Cities under 150,000 population, 142
City, and national party, divorce of, 36; rise of new, 8; short ballot reform in,

40; unification of new, 42, 43

City government, German, 9; *laissez faire,* spirit of, 40; and private business, 47; new division of powers in, 59; publicity in, 59; simpler financial systems in, 60; public hearings, 50.

City government by commission, 268-279; report of National Municipal League on, 268; major features of, 268; a relative success, 268; short ballot in, 269; non-partisan ballot and, 271; initiative and referendum-by-protest and, 271; recall and, 271; abolition of ward lines and, 271; auditor in, 272; civil service commission in, 272; Mayor's veto in, 272; applicability of, to different sized cities, 273; election at large in, 273; size of commission in, in case of large cities, 275; individual commissioners each executive heads of departments in, 276; in cities of over 25,000 population, 278

City hall, 38

City manager, 4; idea of, 8; selection of, and by whom, 62, 82; selection of, in Dayton, 63; selection of, in Springfield, 63; selection of, in Hickory, 63; creation of office of, 76; an appointive officer, 76; qualification of, 76; personal qualifications of, 78; enumerated qualifications of, 78; amount of salaries of, 82; control of commission over, 83; powers of, 83, 90, 91, 93; powers of, in Springfield, 84; a member of board of assessment, 92; tenure of office of, 93; classes appointed by, 96; statutes, 170.

City manager plan of municipal rule, 9; of Dayton, 75; advantages and disadvantages of, 255-262; arguments for, 259-262; advantages of, summarized, 262; arguments against, 262; advantages of Springfield, Ohio, charter summarized, 264; advantages of Dayton, Ohio, charter summarized, 265; cities under, June 1, 1914, 281.

INDEX

City reform, means of accomplishment of, 40
Civic greatness, 4, 9
Code, Virginia section 1038, 2.
Commission, powers of, 62; 68; personnel of, 78; determines salary of city manager, 81
Commission government, of citizens, 9; Royal, 1833, 31; new, 51; old form of, 3, 42; error in, as to commissioners, 52
Commissioners, method of election of, 54; qualifications of, under various charters, 54; term of office of, 55
Conference of Ohio cities, 77
Constitutional Convention of Ohio, 1912, 170
Continent, 9
Councilmen, electing, from wards, 43
Crosby, Hon. John, 3

Dayton, 8, 9; business problem of, 9; fire and police in, 10; bonds of, 11; Bureau of Research in, 11, 12, 127, 132, 282; financial condition of, prior to charter, 11; increased debt of, 13; municipal money of, 13; funds of, unreachable, 13; public corporation of, 14; official reports, 13
Dayton plan, city manager in, 15, 75; initiative and referendum in, 45; recall in, 47; percentage for recall in, 49; commissioners in, term of office of, 55; powers and duties of mayor in, 56; recall of mayor in, 51; salaries of commissioners in, 57; old plan in, 58; civil service boards constituted in, 71; city plan board in, 71; city manager plan, 75; powers of city manager in, 85; location of appointive power in, 95; faults of charter in, 109; fire and police department in, 109; financial department in, 109; budget in, 115; treasurer in, 115; purchasing agent in, 116, 117, 118; provision for money in treasury in, 121; 1913 auditor's reports in, 130, 131; ordinary and extraordinary expenses in, 131; income for 1914 budget in, 132, 136; classification of bud-

get in, 137; details of budget in, 137; administration of cost in budget in, 136; operation of costs in budget in, 136; maintenance of costs in budget in, 137; capital outlay in budget in, 137; advantages of budget in, 139; financial division of manager's report in, 139; department of finance, accounting division in, 140, 141; inventory of city property in, 140; overdrafts impossible in, 141; bookkeeping eliminated in, 141; city budget improved in, 141; more revenues from licenses in, 141; division of receipts and disbursements in, 142; all money in one fund in, 142; bills paid by check in, 142; balances returned to sinking fund in, 142; errors corrected in, 142; division of purchasing in, 143; purchases regulated in, 143; prices reduced in, 143; supplies standardized in, 143; bills discounted in, 143; samples of saving in, 143; reduction of debt in, 144; saving interest charges in, 144

Deal, dollar for dollar, 37

Department, difficulties of connections of divisions of, and commissions, 98; commissioners as head of, 98; in city manager plan, 102; fire and police, 109

Department, health, 10; waterworks, 102; street, 102; treasurer's, 102; law, 102; director of law, 103; duties of director of law, 103; opinion rendered by director of law, 103; suggested division of, law, 104; public service, 104; public service, purpose of, 105; public service, scope of duties of, 105; public welfare, 106; public welfare, scope of, 106; legal aid bureau, 107; public welfare, powers of, 107; public safety, 108; financial, 110, 112; financial, simplicity and uniformity of, 110, 111.

Des Moines plan, 98
Disasters, 9
Dresden, 26

Education, board of, 21
Electorate, power of, 36

INDEX

Emory, Henry Crosby, 194
Employees, political activity of city, 67; method of hiring, 92; in Hickory, N. C., method of hiring, 93
English cities in 18th century, 31
English municipality, chief legal officer of, 32; powers of councils in, 32
English town clerk, 31; powers of, 32; salaries of, 33
Equal pay for equal work, 65; adjustment of salaries to quality of work in, 65
Europe, 4, 24
Executives, controlled, 3, 84

Finance, provisions for funds, 120; certification of funds, 120; money in treasury, 121; measures, 123; income classification, 124; taxes: general, liquor, traffic, cigarettes; licenses: vehicle, venders, theaters and shows, dogs; permits: water and sewer, others; excise taxes: street railways, electric company; markets; city scales; parks; public buildings; workhouses; municipal courts; interest on deposits, 125; public ways, miscellaneous: fire and police, inspection of food products, refund arc lights, sweeping tracks, refunds, cuts and payments, temporary loans, waterworks income, estimated balances; objects of expenditure classification, 125; personal service: salaries and wages, fees and commissions; transportation service, 126; communication service; special contractual service; supplies and material; purchase of land, structures and equipment, 127; fixed charges and contributions, advantages of classification of, 127; official report, 130; ordinary and extraordinary expenses, 131
Foreign ideas, 9
French city government, 34; permanent, professional executives of departments of, 34; *le secretaire de maire* in, 34

Galveston, 3, 4, 5
Galveston plan, 99; evil of

dual functions in commission under, 100
German cities, 24; expert administrator in, 25; municipal officials of, 25; magistrat or Bürgermeister of, 25; administrative council of, 25; city government departments of, 28; council of, 30; municipal budget of, 30.
Gladden, Dr. Washington, 77

Hickory, N. C., 54; commissioners in, term of office of, 55; city manager in, 63; powers of city manager in, 87; city manager plan in, 88; removal power in, 94
Hunt, Mayor, 127

Ideas, progressive, final results of, 50
Indictment, 6
Initiative, 43; in city government, 44; percentage in Dayton, 45; percentage in Springfield, 45
Initiative and referendum, 6, 45

Jefferson, Thomas, 146

Labor, attitude of, and Socialism toward commission manager plan, 155; laboring men elected, 156; laboring man in Dayton commission, 157; laboring man's usefulness in new government, 158; laboring man's advantage in new government, 159; in Springfield campaign, 160; on commission at Springfield, 161; attitude of, in Dayton, 161; resolution of organizations, in Dayton, 162; representation of, in Dayton, 167; Socialism in Dayton, 167; Socialists' attitude in Cleveland and Sandusky, 169
La Grande, Ore., 54; commissioner's term of office in, 55; method of appointment of general manager in, 64; power of general manager in, 89; whom general manager in, appoints, 94
Legislators, powers of, 68
Leipsic, 26
Library of Congress (Division of Bibliography, H. H. B. Mayer, Chief Bibliographer), 292
Lockport, N. Y., plan, city

INDEX

manager in, 21; administrative department in, 21; general and special orders by resolution in, 21; report of condition of departments in, 21; board of estimate and apportionment in, 21; board of audit in, 21; proposal, 22; powers of city manager in, 23; books and vouchers in, 24; first complete city manager plan proposed in, 24; analysis of, plan, 171, 188; short title of, 171; term city in, 172; corporate powers of, 172; application of this act under, 172; adoption of this act under, 172; reorganization under this act, 172; first election under this act, 172; term of first city council, 172; period of reorganization, 173; redistribution of corporate functions, 173; restrictions on such redistributions, 173; succession of functions, 173; no new corporate power, 173; organization within departments, 173; special authority to borrow, 173; election and recall of officers, 173; the city council, 174; citizen's motion, 176; mayor, 180; city manager, 183, 187; department of education, 186; initiative and referendum, 187; duties of city manager, 188; salary of city manager, 188

Lockport, N. Y., proposal, 19; legislature of New York and, 19

Log-rolling, 42

Lynchburg, Va., 80

Magazine articles, 291, 292, 294, 295, 296, 297, 298

Magistrat, character of, 28; power of, 29; character of meeting, 31

Manager, general, of private corporation, 6

Measures, emergency, 68

Miami valley, 8

Military rule, 9

Moore, James Basset, 1

Municipal administration, next to ultimate phase of, 7

Municipal business, regenerative, 15

Municipal government, European method, 9

Municipal management, fallacies in system of, 1; old school of, 73

Municipal rule, arguments for old form of: responsibility to popular will, 256; wards, 256; separation of powers, 257; minorities, 258; essentials, 259

Munro, Prof., 29-34

National Municipal League, 1908 investigation by, of appointees for education of officials, 150; 1912 investigation by, 150

National party and city, divorce of, 36

Officials, education of, 146; problem of, 146; need of, 148; methods of, 148; efforts of institutions toward, 149; courses for, 149; late progress in, 150; problem of systematic course in, 151; in engineering, 151; in law, 151; in medicine, 151; in architecture, 151; in business administration, 151; in finance, 151; graduate work in, 151; probable course in, 151; degrees, 153; practical work in schools in, 153; practical experience in, 153

Officials, subordinate, appointed by Commission, 63

Old government in Dayton, faults of, 10

Old spirit of public officers, 48

Order, old, 3, 6; new, 3

Ordinance, public hearings on tentative budget, 61; publication of, 62; scope of, 69

Parties, 36; emblem at head of ballot, 41

Payroll, certification of, 67

Phœnix, Ariz., 54; method of appointment of General Manager, 64; whom general manager appoints.

Plan, essence of, 4; preliminary, 16; first American manager, 16; Staunton, 16; Galveston, 16; city manager, 3, 42; of Dayton, 75; faults of, remedied, 52, 101

Pledge card, 287; initiative, referendum, protest and recall requested in, 287

Points of view, various, 223-254; of National Municipal League Supplementary Report, Toronto, November, 1913, 223; commission manager variation, 225; definition of commission manager plan, 225; history of commission manager plan, 225; comments, 226; majority report, 227; minority report, Ernest S. Bradford, 232; Foulke, Wm. Dudley, 234; Ashburner, address of, 237; Waite, H. M., statement of, 243; Dayton charter faults, Prof. H. G. James, 249; counter-arguments to objections to Dayton charter, 253

Powers, of commission, 62; limited appointive, 62; legislative, 62; of city manager, 83, 90, 91, 92; of director of finance, 111

Prendergast, Wm. A., 123

Probationary period, 64

Professional idea, 2; in English city government, 32; in France, 34

Prussian cities, 24

Purchase of supplies, old system for, 118; evils of, 119; new systems of, advantages of, 120

Purchasing agent, duties of, 116; advantages of, 117; payment for supplies to, 117; city manager approves action of, 118; in Staunton and Springfield, 118

Question, Dayton, 9

Recall, 6; in Dayton, 47; dangers of, 48; period of immunity from, 49; Springfield provision concerning, 50

Referendum, 45; details of plans, 46; percentage in plans, 46

Results, 194-222; financial savings, 195; economical reorganization of departments, 196; character of work of officials, 197; financial reorganization, 197; public works, 198; purchasing agent savings, 199; health department, 199; new method of financing bond issue, 199; report of results in Dayton, 201; staff conferences, 201; expenditures limited by income, 201; eight-hour day, 201; grade elimination, 201; building code, 202; better street car service, 202; civic plan board, 202; civic music, 202; renaming and renumbering streets,

202; life-saving equipment, 202; crossing blockades, 202; Civic Workers' League, 203; traffic rules, 203; additional water, 203; garbage removal, 203; sewers, 203; park system, 204; petty offenders, 204; Department of Law, 204; settlement of complaints, 204; loan sharks' campaign, 204; parole of workhouse prisoners, 205; mail order frauds, 205; home rule, 205; general statement, 205; salary saving of $27,000, 205; office of Director, 205; Department of Public Service, 205; expediting public works, 206; permits simplified, 206; future refuse disposal, 206; Division of Engineering, 206; investigation of sewers, 206; efficient street inspection, 206; Island Park bridge, 207; $12,000 saving on Valley Street bridge, 207; Division of Streets, 207; street oiling, 207; refuse collection, 207; garbage collection, 207; dead animals, 207; street flushing, 208; for cleaner streets, 208; street repairs, 208; service cuts, 209; improvement of dumps, 209; Division of Water, 209; increased water pressure, 209; additional water supply, 209; improved pumping, 210; plans for water improvements, 210; Dayton View supply, 210; reduced coal consumption, 211; meter repairs, 211; a waterworks superintendent, 211; Division of Public Lands and Buildings, 211; municipal garage, 211; alterations in City Building, 212; saving on heat, 212; Department of Public Welfare, 212; Division of Health, 212; full time health officer, 212; new quarters, 212; reorganization of health work, 212; public health nursing, 213; vacant property, 213; insanitary conditions, 213; lower baby death rate, 213; three public clinics, 214; Division of Parks, 214; McCabe's Park, 214; McKinley Park, 214; Island Park, 214; community gardens, 215; Division of

INDEX

Recreation, 216; reorganization of playground work, 216; number of playgrounds doubled, 216; new equipment secured, 216; play tournaments, 217; Division of Correction, 217; workhouse overhauled, 217; police station, 218; cost records installed, 217; workhouse labor, 218; municipal lodging house established, 219; the city garden, 219; Division of Legal Aid, 219; free legal advice, 219; Division of Charities, 220; city infirmary abolished, 220; report of public safety, 220; investigation of fire and police service, 220; report of police, 221; more police, 221; women probation officers, 221; school for police, 221; uniforms and drills, 221; traffic rules, 221; report of fire, 221; fire prevention, 221; service tests, 222; motor apparatus, 222
Roosevelt, Theo., 36

Shame of a city, 11
Solution, 7
Springfield, Ohio, plan, 113; initiative percentage, 45; drafting of initiative ordinance in, 45; recall in, 50; commissioners in, term of office of, 55; selection of city manager in, 63; compensation of civil service boards in, 68; provision for advisory boards in, 70; powers of city manager in, 84; whom appointed by city manager, 94; purchasing agent, 118
Staunton, Va., population of, 16; controlled executive plan in, 20
Staunton, Va., plan, finance, education and legislation in, 17; manager in, salary of, 17; supervisor of department superintendents in, 17; purchasing agent in, 17, 118; powers of manager in, 18; expenditures in, 18; president of common council in, 18; productive saloon license in, 19; city manager idea in, 19
System, merit, 10; of patronage, 42; municipal judiciary, 63

Tables and charts, 12
Taney, Chief Justice, 170

Taylor, Frederick Winslow, 73
Taylor, Hannis, 98
Test, the, 38; ultimate, of fitness as candidate, 38
Treasurer, city, 115
Treaty-making of factionalism, 42
Trustees, of sinking fund, 67; of public trusts, 71
Turning point, the, 9

University, Harvard, Bureau of Research of, 149-150; Graduate School of, 149
University of Texas, Bureau of Research of, 150; School of Government of, 150; Bureau of, under James, Herman G., 150
University of Virginia, 147

Virginia Statute, 189-192; general councilmanic plan in, 189; modified commission plan in, 190; city manager plan in, 191; provisions applicable to each plan in, 192

Waite, H. M., City Manager, 14; career of, 79
Wards, 42; abolition of, 54
Washington, George, 6
Wilson, Woodrow, 1
Woodruff, Clinton Rogers, 51

(2)

METROPOLITAN AMERICA

AN ARNO PRESS COLLECTION

Adams, Thomas. **The Design of Residential Areas:** Basic Considerations, Principles, and Methods. (Harvard City Planning Studies, Vol. VI). 1934.

Anderson, Wilbert L. **The Country Town:** A Study of Rural Evolution. 1906.

Arnold, Bion J. **Report on the Improvement and Development of the Transportation Facilities of San Francisco.** Submitted to the Mayor and the Board of Supervisors, City of San Francisco. March, 1913. 1913.

Association for the Improvement of the Condition of the Poor. **Housing Conditions in Baltimore.** Report of a Special Committee of the Association for the Improvement of the Condition of the Poor and the Charity Organization Society. Submitting the Results of an Investigation Made by Janet E. Kemp. 1907.

Bassett, Edward M. **Zoning:** The Laws, Administration, and Court Decisions During the First Twenty Years. 1936.

Bauer, Catherine. **Modern Housing.** 1934.

Case, Walter H. **History of Long Beach and Vicinity.** (Volume 1). 1927.

Chamberlin, Everett. **Chicago and Its Suburbs.** 1874.

Chapin, E[dwin] H[ubbell]. **Humanity in the City.** 1854.

Coit, Stanton. **Neighborhood Guilds:** An Instrument of Social Reform. 1891.

Comey, Arthur C[oleman]. **Transition Zoning.** (Harvard City Planning Studies, Vol. V). 1933.

Covington, Kentucky, City Planning and Zoning Commission. **Comprehensive Plan for Covington, Kentucky, and Environs.** [1932].

Goodnow, Frank J. **City Government in the United States.** 1910.

Hinman, Albert Greene. **Population Growth and Its Demands Upon Land for Housing in Evanston, Illinois.** 1931.

Hubbard, Theodora Kimball and Henry Vincent Hubbard. **Our Cities To-Day and To-Morrow:** A Survey of Planning and Zoning Progress in the United States. 1929.

Kellogg, Paul Underwood, editor. **The Pittsburgh District Civic Frontage** (Pittsburgh Survey, Vol. 5). 1914.

Kellogg, Paul Underwood, editor. **Wage-Earning Pittsburgh** (Pittsburgh Survey, Vol. 6). 1914.

Knowles, Morris. **Industrial Housing:** With Discussion of Accompanying Activities; Such as Town Planning, Street Systems, Development of Utility Services, and Related Engineering and Construction Features. 1920.

Lindsey, Ben B. and Rube Borough. **The Dangerous Life.** 1931.

Marsh, Benjamin Clarke. **An Introduction to City Planning:** Democracy's Challenge to the American City. With a Chapter on the Technical Phases of City Planning by George B. Ford. [1909].

Maxwell, Sidney D. **The Suburbs of Cincinnati:** Sketches, Historical and Descriptive. 1870.

Metropolitan Police Manuals—1871, 1913. Introduction by Richard C. Wade. 1974.

Moehlman, Arthur B. **Public Education in Detroit.** 1925.

National Municipal League. Committee on Metropolitan Government. **The Government of Metropolitan Areas in the United States.** Prepared by Paul Studenski with the Assistance of the Committee on Metropolitan Government. 1930.

National Resources Committee. **Our Cities:** Their Role in the National Economy. Report of the Urbanism Committee to the National Resources Committee. 1937.

New York City. Board of Aldermen. Committee on General Welfare. **Preliminary Report of the Committee on General Welfare in the Matter of a Request of the Conference of Organized Labor Relative to Educational Facilities.** Meeting of June 26, 1917. 1917.

New York City. Staten Island Improvement Commission. **Report of a Preliminary Scheme of Improvements.** 1871.

Ogburn, William F. **Social Characteristics of Cities:** A Basis for New Interpretations of the Role of the City in American Life. 1937.

Pink, Louis H. **The New Day in Housing.** 1928.

Powell, Hickman. **Ninety Times Guilty.** 1939.

Regional Plan Association. **From Plan to Reality.** 1933/1938/1942. 3 volumes in one.

Regional Plan of New York and Its Environs. 2 volumes. 1929/1931.

Regional Survey of New York and Its Environs. 10 volumes. 1927-1931.

Simonds, Thomas C. **History of South Boston;** Formerly Dorchester Neck, Now Ward XII of the City of Boston. 1857.

Smythe, William E. **City Homes on Country Lanes:** Philosophy and Practice of the Home-in-a-Garden. 1921.

Straus, Nathan. **The Seven Myths of Housing.** 1944.

Studies of Suburbanization in Connecticut. Numbers 1-3. 1936/1938/1939.

Toulmin, Harry Aubrey, Jr. **The City Manager:** A New Profession. 1916.

U.S. Public Health Service. **Municipal Health Department Practice for the Year 1923.** Based Upon Surveys of the 100 Largest Cities in the United States Made by the United States Public Health Service in Cooperation with the Committee on Administrative Practice, American Public Health Association. Public Health Bulletin No. 164. 1926.

U.S. Senate. Committee on the District of Columbia. **City Planning.** Hearing Before the Committee on the District of Columbia, United States Senate, on the Subject of City Planning. 61st Congress, 2nd Session, Senate Document No. 422. 1910.

U.S. Senate. Juvenile Court of the District of Columbia. **Message from the President of the United States Transmitting a Letter from the Judge of the Juvenile Court of the District of Columbia Submitting a Report Covering the Work of the Juvenile Court During the Period From July 1, 1906, to June 30, 1926.** 69th Congress, 2nd Session, Senate Document No. 236. 1927.

Upson, Lent D. **Practice of Municipal Administration.** 1926.

West Side Studies. Carried on Under the Direction of Pauline Goldmark. 1914. 2 volumes in one.

Wilcox, Delos Flranklin l. **Great Cities in America:** Their Problems and Their Government. 1910.

Zueblin, Charles. **American Municipal Progress.** 1916.